Language, Learners and Computers

Human intelligence and artificial unintelligence

John Higgins

Longman

London and New York

Longman Group UK Limited
Longman House, Burnt Mill, Harlow,
Essex CM20 2JE, England
and Associated Companies throughout the world.

Published in the United States of America by
Longman Inc., New York

First published 1988
Reprinted 1988

BRITISH LIBRARY CATALOGUING IN PUBLICATION DATA
Higgins, John, *1939–*
    Language, learners and computers: human
    intelligence and artificial unintelligence.
    1. Language and languages — Computer-
    assisted instruction
    I. Title
    407′.8   P53

LIBRARY OF CONGRESS CATALOGING IN PUBLICATION DATA
Higgins, John, 1939 Apr. 14–
    Language, learners and computers.
    Bibliography: p. 104
    Includes index.
    1. Language and languages — Computer-assisted
    instruction.   I. Title.
    P53.28.H5   1988   418′.007′8   87-3794

Set in Linotron 202 Erhardt 10/12pt.

Produced by Longman Singapore Publishers (Pte) Ltd.
Printed in Singapore

ISBN 0-582-55263-X

Contents

Note

The words *magister* and *pedagogue* are used throughout this book in a special sense, which is defined on pages 12 to 15.

Introduction: Magister and pedagogue

If you present somebody with an oval outline of a head and ask them to fill in the eyes, the chances are that they will draw something like this:

dividing the head in the proportion of one third to two thirds. A child will tend to put the eyes even higher. Ask a trained artist to do the same thing, however, and he or she will almost certainly do it this way:

dividing the head into even halves. This is a good deal closer to what we really look like. The interesting question is how the artist, or rather the community of artists, knows this. The location of the eyes is not self-evident, since getting it right depends on having specially acute observation or else on training in one specific activity rather than general intelligence or education. Most of us are seduced by the closeness of the eyes to the hairline into thinking they are much higher on the head than they really are. The artist, having attempted to represent reality in another medium, has found out, either by trial and error or through training, where the eyes belong.

When we try to use computers in education, we could be said to be transferring acts of teaching and learning to a new medium. Like the child or the untrained layman, our first attempts will reflect our preconceptions or common-sense ideas about learning. But the machine and the results we obtain with its aid will not allow us to get away with failure. When a predicted learning event does not take place, we are forced to conclude either that the machine is unsuitable, or that our model of how to use it was based on a misconception. If we examine the second of these explanations, we may, like the artist, gain new insights about the nature of teaching and learning from our attempts.

What is knowledge?

Metaphors are devices which we use to understand one thing in terms of another; for example, we understand time better when we divide it into units like those of length. In education, however, we may be hamstrung by lack of a suitable metaphor for the stuff of education: information, knowledge, insights, understanding. I used the word 'stuff', which is a commodity metaphor, but this is highly misleading. When you give away a commodity, such as land or money or even time, your own holding is diminished. But when you share information or understanding, you do not lose any of what you have. On the contrary, as Seneca told us nearly two thousand years ago, 'People learn even while they teach.' (*Homines dum docent discunt.*) The lack of a suitable metaphor for information underlies the tangles of copyright legislation and the flagrant piracy which bedevils the computer and video industries. Plagiarism and piracy are, of course, a form of theft, since they deprive creative people and their publishers of income. But they do not feel like theft, since no one appears to have lost anything. We simply do not know how to put a price on information or conduct transactions with it, and so continue to treat it as if it were soap powder.

Empty vessels

The commonest model of the education process is one which uses the inappropriate commodity metaphor. It is often called the empty-vessel model. It assumes two parties, a knower and a learner; learning occurs when the knower expounds or describes some knowledge and the learner attends to the exposition. Knowledge is poured from the full vessel into the empty one. Under this model, all failures can be attributed to the communication stage. Either the knower has expounded inadequately, or the learner has been inattentive. Teacher training, therefore, can concentrate on improving the quality of the exposition, making it simpler and clearer, or on securing the continued alertness of the learner by, for instance, having frequent informal tests of recall, or by switching between different types of activity and modes of response.

However naive this model may seem, it has considerable common-sense validity and pervades our thinking and talking about learning. ('How many times have I got to tell you. . .?') It is a very adequate description of some of the day-to-day acts of instruction which we need to carry out: a librarian explaining library regulations to a new reader, or an instruction manual describing the operation of a machine to its purchaser, for instance. The inadequacy of the model is exposed not so much by educational failure as by educational success. It contains no explanation of how pupils can come to exceed in skill or comprehension the masters who have taught them.

And yet such pupils exist; without them the transmission of education would be a process of continuous attrition. One of the clearest examples is language learning. Many millions of people are engaged in learning second languages, often from teachers who are not native speakers. A number of these learners will come to command a level of skill which may exceed that of their teachers and which, in any case, cannot be described in the time available to the teacher for exposition. Indeed the skills of a competent (not necessarily native) speaker of a language go beyond what can be adequately described by academic linguists in lifetimes of study.

I remember one particular case when I was giving language tests in Thailand. The candidates were 18-year-old school-leavers, and one of them was outstanding; his pronunciation was almost perfect, he made very few errors, and he had a rich vocabulary and a wide range of idioms. I looked at his record, but could find nothing to explain it; he had attended an ordinary Bangkok school and had never been abroad. I wondered if he had been lucky enough to have a native speaker as a teacher, so I asked him who his teachers had been. 'My teachers?' he answered, 'My teachers were Laurence Olivier, Vivien Leigh, Richard Burton and Gregory Peck.' I shall return in Chapter 4 to the sense in which these film stars were his 'teachers'; meanwhile here was a pupil who already spoke better English than ninety per cent of the English teachers in the Thai education system.

Mass instruction

The earliest embodiments of computer-assisted learning made use of a model which was, for all its elaboration, a version of the empty-vessel theory. These early experiments provided a very good test bed for the model, since the machines could eliminate many of the drawbacks of mass instruction where one teacher attempts to serve a dozen to a hundred learners simultaneously. The machines could provide individually paced exposition and individually monitored testing. The evaluation studies of the various projects did not show either dramatic success or dramatic failure; in most cases there were either trivial gains reported or erratic results which were difficult to interpret without some measures of the personalities and attitudes of the learners. (For a review of the evaluation literature see Higgins 1983a.) The implication of these results has perhaps not been well appreciated: it is that we can no longer blame mass instruction for educational failure. The problem with education is not the problem of having too few knowers to serve all the potential learners on a one-to-one basis.

There are of course competitors to the empty-vessel theory, theories which assume that learners bring mental structures and procedures to the learning process which make them active negotiators rather than passive participants in learning. There have also been enthusiastic promoters of computer applications which embody such theories and seek to validate and extend them. One thinks in particular of Seymour Papert, a disciple of Piaget, and his book *Mindstorms* (1980), and of the vast amount of work using the LOGO language which has flowed from his work. Such developments are hard to evaluate in conventional ways (since many evaluation instruments are themselves firmly rooted in empty-vessel theory), but the anecdotal accounts of their success are sufficient to have galvanized the teaching profession into excitement and effort on a large scale. Second-language learning, however, was not initially part of this effort, and it is only fairly recently that any use has been made of computers for language learning which did not have an explicit or implicit base in empty-vessel theory. The little innovative work that has been done is not grounded on a single theory of learning, although it may call on generative linguistics, discourse analysis, classroom interaction studies, or Krashen's Monitor Model for a partial justification. The evidence in its favour, such as it is, remains anecdotal.

What I want to do in this book is to look at this anecdotal evidence and to account for it in terms of a different metaphor for the teacher/knower and two possible roles that he or she can take up, which I call *magister* and *pedagogue*. The outcome will not amount to a theory of language learning but may provide some explanations for the success or failure of certain techniques. If it does, its relevance will not be confined to the computer itself or to the schools which use them; there may be implications which are just as relevant for learners and teachers who have no machines. This book, therefore, is not in any sense a 'how-to' guide to the process of using computers to teach. It is, instead, an account of what we may see when we look in the mirror, studying the way we create and use computer programs in the one specific area of language learning.

Overview

In the first chapter, I shall look at the balance of initiatives and ask which member of the teacher/learner pair takes control in various types of activity. I develop this into the metaphor representing two roles for the teacher, the *magister* who initiates and controls, and the *pedagogue* who responds and serves. In particular, I shall be looking at some common misunderstandings of these roles, and at the temptation to 'think magisterially' about tasks and events in which such thinking is inappropriate.

The second chapter examines the nature of linguistic 'command', admitting that we know very little about the processes which turn our exposure to language into the ability to use language. Variability among learners is often explained by differences in motivation, but this explanation begs many questions. I suggest that the circumstances of mass instruction tend to increase variability in learning performance by sometimes suppressing learning instincts, and that computers have shown us what happens when learners are guided to or are able to find their 'optimal challenge'.

In the third chapter, I look at ways in which the natural exploratory instincts of the learner can be brought into play in second-language learning. This is illustrated with a number of techniques which reverse normal teacher/student roles by requiring the student to experiment, to take initiatives, or to 'teach' a machine. It is in this kind of activity that the computer can be most useful; it does not, however, need to be elaborately programmed or to be made 'artificially intelligent'.

The fourth chapter deals with the teacher and his or her roles as manager, knower and model, motivator, and diagnostician. I suggest that teachers are valuable in a magisterial role and carry it out skilfully, but need to recognize the occasions when they should withdraw and become pedagogues. I take one step back and ask not only what lessons there are in the magister/pedagogue distinction for learning, but also for teacher training, and ask how teachers can be trained in the use of computers.

The fifth chapter examines learning materials, traditionally in print form, but now often using a variety of other media. Many textbooks embody magisterial assumptions, particularly those which seek to be 'teacher-proof', and I contrast these with reading anthologies and other materials which are presented as resources. I examine the effect of the medium, paper or screen, on the content, and describe the kind of material which exploits both the medium and the pedagogue role.

The sixth chapter deals with measurement and evaluation, an area in which the ELT profession is currently floundering without an adequate theory. How can one measure abilities which are gained from a still unknown mixture of conscious and unconscious processes, and which show themselves in overt performance which provides only an erratic reflection of the learner's covert competence? Although I have no easy answer to this question, I suggest that one benefit of the computer is to make learners more interested in knowing their own ability and therefore to make them into enthusiastic test-takers and test-analysers. In an institutional context a test is seen as adversarial, whereas in the hands of a pedagogue it can be both entertainment and tool.

The final chapter looks at the problems of technology, and compares the way that computers and language laboratories have affected teachers and learners. I suggest that the computer's main value is as an environment which allows language experiments to be carried out. However, any teaching scheme which allows or encourages trial-and-error learning must also respect the intelligence of the learners; if it does not, the fear of making errors will wipe out what one learns from the trials.

Here and there I shall describe computer programs and their effects on learners, but such accounts are included only for the bearing they have on the question of how learners learn. While it would be foolish to cast aside a mechanical aid where it can be of value, I have never recommended any kind of massive transfer of resources into computer-aided learning. You cannot solve problems by throwing money and machinery at them; you solve them, rather, by finding out what causes them.

What I do recommend, however, is that teachers should look carefully at what computers can do, and should be ready on occasion to think like a computer or even to pretend to be a computer. In the process we may learn what we really do when we think like a human being. It is sad that the stereotype of a language class often seems to contain a teacher who behaves like a human being and forty learners who behave like machines. By increasing our own understanding of machines, we may be able to let learners behave more like human beings again.

Acknowledgements

This is a very personal book, and the main source of the ideas in it is the students and colleagues I have worked with over the last twenty-five years. I have kept to a minimum the number of scholarly citations; where I have knowingly used somebody's work as the basis of my own, I acknowledge the source, but I do not feel the need to refer to the work of every scholar who might agree or disagree with some point I am making.

I began using the slave metaphor in relation to computer-assisted language learning in a position paper prepared for my British Council colleagues in June 1981, which was distributed under the title 'CALL: the nature of the interaction'. I introduced the terms *magister* and *pedagogue* in a talk given at a meeting of TESOL Portugal in Lisbon in April 1983, the text of which appeared under the title 'Can computers teach?' in *Calico Journal*, 1, 2, in September 1983, reprinted in *English Teaching Forum* in July 1985. The theme was developed in a paper 'Learning with computers', which appeared in *Teaching and the Teacher*, MEP 1984 (Proceedings of the 1984 Bologna Conference).

Material from Chapters 3 and 4 was printed in papers which I contributed to the sixth GREDIL conference, Quebec, 1985, and to the twentieth TESOL convention, Anaheim, March 1986. Many of the ideas in Chapter 5 were developed during a seminar in 1984 in which I was collaborating with Branka Panić of the Centre for Foreign Languages, Belgrade.

The influence of Tim Johns of Birmingham University is pervasive. I am specially grateful to Sue Fortescue, formerly of Eurocentres, whose detailed comments led to great improvements, and I have also had useful comments from Charles Alderson, Kurt Moench and Penny McCahill at Lancaster University. I am also grateful to Mario Rinvolucri who, both in published work and in private conversation, has triggered much of the thinking which has resulted in this book. My wife, Muriel, has been a source of ideas as well as of practical feedback and support.

I do not, of course, expect anyone mentioned here to agree with everything I say or to take responsibility for any statement.

1 The metaphor

A shopkeeper once put notices in his shop-window saying *Ici on parle français*, *Man spricht deutsch*, and *Se habla español*. When a friend saw these, he said, 'I didn't know you spoke all these languages, Bert.' 'I don't,' replied the shopkeeper. 'Well, who does then?' 'My customers.'

Imagine a game played by two players who sit back to back or, in some way, out of sight but within earshot of each other. Each has a game board consisting of a sixteen by sixteen grid of squares. On player A's board, and only on that one, some of the lines have been thickened to create a maze. Each thickened line represents an impassable barrier.

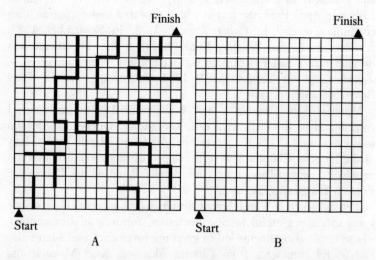

Player B's task is to move a token from, say, the bottom left square to the top right in as few turns as possible. The method of moving is to call out a number of squares and a direction, e.g. 'Five squares right'. Player A now announces if that move is legal, i.e. if it does not cross a thickened line. If it is, and only then, player B makes the move. (Player A must also mirror the move on his own board so that he knows where the next move will start.) If the move is not legal the tokens stay where they are but the turn is counted against B's score.

Let us further assume that player B may not mark his board in any way. He has to rely on inference and memory to work out the route. Player A acts purely as informant and arbiter, and cannot influence the outcome of the game. In this form of the game there is very little interest or fun for A but quite a lot for B. What is more, by playing repeatedly with the same maze B can improve his performance as he gradually memorizes the locations of the barriers, and if he plays with different mazes he will probably find himself evolving search strategies which lead to better overall success rates. He will develop a feel for the kind of routes that are likely to work.

Roles

We could allow A a more active role, say as adviser. He could now say things like 'There are a lot of obstructions towards the middle of the board; better keep to the edges.' The trouble with this is that the boundaries of such general advice are fuzzy, and A would not know when such advice was necessary or wanted, or whether it had been helpful. However, it would serve to equalize the contributions, and therefore the enjoyment, of the two players. We could go even further and let A give specific instructions, 'Move two squares up, then four right . . .', until the optimum route had been announced. B's role is now confined to executing these instructions. This maximizes A's part in the game, and therefore his enjoyment, but, since he has full sight of the board, his task is still much less interesting than the task originally set to B. Meanwhile B's activity has been turned into something very mechanical and boring. One consequence is that there will be no point in playing the game more than once for each form of maze, and that B will end each round without any mental visualization of the board that A has been using.

Time

Another consequence is that the game will be over much more quickly. This could be presented as an advantage, or at least as a necessity imposed by time constraints. 'We've got twenty of these mazes to do in the next hour. I haven't got time to listen to your wrong guesses.' The game has now been turned into a duty or a chore, but if player B is obliged by social convention to play it, he may well accept this explanation and settle to the task of moving his counter over twenty prescribed routes.

Teaching and learning

By now it should be obvious, from the context in which you are reading this, that I intend the game to be an analogy of the learning/teaching process. Like all analogies it over-simplifies a complex process, and nothing can be proved with it. It leaves out a great deal. I have, for instance, said nothing about how B comes to know the rules of the game, whether A has taught him, or both have been taught by C, or whether the rules are part of their shared cultural background. I have not said who draws the mazes, though evidently this cannot be B. I have not said why A and B are playing, although I have suggested that it is for enjoyment. Languages, though, are not learned just for enjoyment but for practical use in communication. The process of learning to move a counter across a grid under the constraints of arbitrary rules is clearly not an accurate model of the process of mastering anything as complex in structure, in origins and in application as a natural language.

Dichotomies

What the game analogy does suggest, however, is the way in which we tend to think about teaching and learning in simple black-and-white oppositions. In recent years we have been presented with an abundance of dichotomies: control versus freedom, accuracy versus fluency, teacher-centred versus learner-centred approaches, conscious *learning* versus unconscious *acquisition*, and formal versus informal learning (see, for instance, Brumfit 1983, Krashen 1982, Ellis 1985). In many of these discussions evidence is presented that something important is lost when the teacher says 'This is the way to do it'; learners get bored or fail to transfer learning to life. So why do teachers go on saying it?

Mass instruction

In a classroom situation they have to, at least for a part of the time. Imagine player A's problem if he has to respond to thirty different player Bs, all simultaneously clamouring for rulings. He is almost bound to say at some point, 'Shut up all of you and do what I tell you.' Could we get round the problem by having learners work in groups or pairs? To continue the analogy, we could have the various player Bs taking turns to go up to player A and then collaborating by pooling the knowledge they have acquired. But, even if we grant that the mazes they are trying to explore are identical, this is still a makeshift. One may say to another 'This is how I got here' or 'I tried that and it didn't work', but these pieces of help depend on a very partial view of the maze and on possibly imperfect recollection. However accurate they may be, the other member of the partnership cannot rely on them as he can on player A's sight of the board.

Exploratory learning

In spite of the over-simplification, the game analogy and the exploration metaphor underlying it describe a process which is very familiar to the parents of a toddler learning its first language. The caretaker, i.e. the parent, playgroup teacher or baby-sitter, is sometimes treated like a puzzle to be solved. New utterances are tried out to see if they work and, if they do not work the first time, are repeated louder and more reproachfully while the caretaker casts around trying to understand what the child wants. Both sides try to modify what they say until there is a breakthrough and the message is understood. Once a child has found out how to formulate questions, it often goes through a phase of asking questions continually. There is no coherent line to the questioning. Anything which enters the field of consciousness is tackled as it is perceived, and discarded the moment something looms larger. The child does not seem particularly grateful for the answers or even very interested; it just asks more questions.

When you learn a foreign language you do not normally let yourself behave like this, partly because you have already learned rules of conversational behaviour, one of which is 'be relevant'. However, a pattern of activity rather like that of the toddler is used in some of the so-called fringe methodologies, notably Community Language Learning (CLL) and the Silent Way. In CLL any member of the group of learners can start an exchange in any way they please, calling on the teacher to help them express the utterance in the foreign language. In the Silent Way the learners have the task of communicating with a teacher who, apart from a tiny initial demonstration, refuses to speak at all, responding only with nods and shakes or by moving coloured blocks around. This puts the learner in a position similar to that of the toddler trying to make its parent understand what it wants.

The machine as teacher

The conventional labels for player A and player B are 'teacher' and 'learner'. These labels, however, are overlaid with associations gathered from centuries of mass education in institutions, places where the teacher is a salaried and trained authority figure. Inevitably, when computers began to be developed with enough flexibility and sophistication to be used for education, it was the role of 'teacher' that was assigned to the machine. This was in spite of considerable and understandable emotional resistance to the idea of a machine replacing a human being. Much was written in the sixties and seventies claiming that the machine was only an auxiliary whose main task would be to take over tasks that human teachers (namely the trained professionals) could not handle, in particular individual work with students who had special goals or severe remedial needs. It was also claimed that the machine would handle the tedious tasks of drilling, releasing the teacher for creative work in free forms of activity such as discussion. None of this clamorous defence could conceal the reality that what those early computer programs were doing was presenting facts, setting exercise tasks, and evaluating responses. They were definitely cast as player A in his most active and interfering role.

Magister

Since I would like to reserve the word 'teacher' for a wider use, I have had to coin a special term for player A when he takes over this directive function, when he tells player B where to move. I call him *magister*. He (the classical nomenclature is my excuse for the masculine pronoun) wears an academic gown to show that he is qualified in subject knowledge. Visible in his top pocket is his salary cheque,

symbolizing the security of tenured appointment. In one hand he holds a handkerchief, symbol of the care and concern which (we hope) he feels for individual learners. In the other he carries a cane, symbolizing his authority to evaluate, praise and censure. In front of him is the book, the symbol of the order of events, the structure which is imposed on him by the syllabus makers and which he will impose on the learners by means of the lesson plan.

The machine as magister

The computer is very good at performing some of the typical activities of a magister, and very poor at others. It is good at presenting statements and illustrating them with examples, since it can continue drawing on a store of ready-made examples or assembling random examples from a substitution table for a period which would outlast the patience of a human. Similarly it can continue with a questioning sequence or repeat explanations beyond the point where humans would lose their tempers. But it is poor at assessing answers, since it cannot store every wrong answer that might be given and make an appropriate response to each, nor can it judge the reason for a particular wrong answer, whether carelessness, faulty grasp of a principle, sheer perversity or, perhaps, experiment. It is very poor indeed at conveying enthusiasm or showing love, whether love of the learner or love of the subject matter.

The human as magister

At this point the simplicity of my original maze-game metaphor breaks down, since it suggests that magisterial teaching is always wrong. After all, in the game it destroys the point of the activity. In practice, however, magisterial teaching can often be what is demanded and needed. It is as if player B asks to be 'talked through' a few mazes as preparation for the time when he starts to solve them without help. In the same way learners will often demand a structured order to events or a magisterial exposition of new matter. They may rightly scorn the teacher who says 'What would you like to do now?' and respond 'You tell us; you're the expert' or 'Why haven't you prepared a lesson?'

Human teachers, therefore, assume the magisterial role, not only because it is forced on us by the circumstances of mass teaching, but also because it is sometimes right. Several millenia of experience with it have made us fairly good at it. The best teachers have enthusiasm and can communicate a love of their subject. They are highly sensitive to student needs and flexible in their responses to need. But even this flexibility may not redeem entirely the loss of autonomy that player B, the learner, suffers when the teacher tells him what to do next. If I wanted to learn a game, say chess, I would probably read a book or attend lessons which explicitly taught the rules rather than try to deduce the rules by watching or joining in a game in progress. I would be ready, at that stage, to accept authority and to adopt a purely responsive role, answering questions rather than asking them. I would need a magister and would accept a person, a book, or even a computer in that role. Sooner or later, however, I would become discontented with the magister and would want to take on a more active role for myself. In the case of learning to play chess it would not be hard for me to do this, but in many curricular subjects the pleasure of 'playing the game' may be deferred for an unreasonable length of time.

Pedagogue

Let us think of a different kind of teacher, the assistant, often young and only partly trained, a native speaker of the language his students are learning, visiting their country mainly to improve his own grasp of their language. His classes are often labelled 'Conversation' and are not part of the examined syllabus. Lesson time with him is unstructured, since he has not had the training to conduct magisterial teaching. He may well function just as informant: 'Tell us about food, marriage, pop music, the police . . . in your country.' Or he may entertain with songs, with talks and reading aloud, or with games.

The obvious way in which we can computerize the functions of an assistant is in language games. But again it is worth looking at the underlying image we have of the games-playing computer and of the assistant. The name I have for this kind of teacher is *pedagogue*, a word which originally meant 'the slave who escorts the children to school'. So think of a man in sandals and a cheap cotton robe, walking five paces behind the young master. He carries the young master's books for him, but no cane. The young master snaps his fingers and the pedagogue approaches. He answers the young master's questions, recites a poem, translates words, plays a game, or even, if that is what the young master demands, gives a test. The young master snaps his fingers again, and the pedagogue goes back to his place. He hopes he has given satisfaction, since otherwise he may starve.

The language assistant and the au pair girl are the last survivors of a pedagogue tradition that stretches from classical times, through the private tutors employed by wealthy families and the ballet and fencing masters attached to aristocratic courts, to their much diminished role nowadays. *Pedagogue* is no longer a career. We cannot afford pedagogues, and we have a bad conscience about slavery and the exploitation of people in menial roles. Instead we use libraries or, increasingly, computerized information systems. One of the clearest ways in which we have given machines the slave role is in word-processing; the computer becomes the scribe, copying out the master's words neatly but not daring to alter them, though it may raise a tentative question about spelling or even grammar. We seem, however, to have lost the knack that we once possessed of exploiting pedagogues, of asking questions and making demands on a slave without stopping to ask if the demands were reasonable. Such behaviour may be despicable towards another human being. It is surely reasonable when your slave is made of transistors and plastic.

Curiously enough, one of the consequences of employing a slave is that one has to do the slave's thinking. When a slave is trained to give unquestioning obedience, it becomes the master's responsibility to think out the task in advance and to give effective orders. Many people who have employed servants or supervised junior office staff have tales to tell of instructions which have been obeyed literally, often with comic or disastrous results. Typical is the account of the junior clerk, sent to cash a large cheque and asked, on his way out, to 'bring back some parking meter change'. He returns several hours later with sacks of coins. The computer behaves to a great extent like this clerk, and it is the user who must develop the skill of anticipation and exact description of a task.

Programmed learning

The pioneers of computer-assisted learning never considered giving the machine any role other than magister. They saw teaching as a process of dialogue between teachers and learners, and looked only for ways of enabling their limited and basically stupid machines to conduct the teacher's side. They found the solution in the system known as Programmed Learning (PL). PL fitted well into two prevailing orthodoxies of the fifties, behaviourist learning psychology and structural linguistics. Underlying PL is a belief that a body of knowledge can be reduced to a set of very small steps, each of which can be expressed in a brief verbal message and is easily learnable. Each step is turned into a frame which contains a small amount of exposition, followed by a question or task. The learner attempts the task, checks the answer and proceeds to the next frame (or, in the case of branching or Crowderian PL, is directed via a multiple-choice format towards the next appropriate frame). PL does not in fact need a computer or any other machinery; it can be used just as effectively in paper forms, and computers used exclusively for PL are sometimes known disparagingly as 'page-turners'. The real magister is not the machine but the person who wrote the material and imagined the kind of conversation he or she might have with an imaginary student. It is this displaced magister who is doing the initiating, task setting and evaluating; the machine is merely the medium for transmitting the script.

Machine worship

In our general awe of modern science and of computers, it is easy to forget that a computer is essentially a responsive device. It does not naturally initiate; it does not want to talk to you. Forgetting for a moment the complex logging-on sequences which one must go through with a time-shared mainframe or mini, the word it often displays when you switch on is READY. From that point it is waiting for you to use whatever may be in its memory. It will only pose questions or demand responses if a programmer has created a program which makes it do so. Responding to and obeying the machine's commands ought to be a deliberate and temporary act of will on our part, something we agree to do because we anticipate some satisfaction from it. There are dangers if we forget this and fall into an inappropriate pattern of respect towards the machine.

The man who has appreciated these dangers and has written on them most cogently is Joseph Weizenbaum. In his book *Computer power and human reason* (1976) he takes as his starting point the reactions on the part of colleagues and laymen towards his famous program ELIZA. ELIZA, written in 1966, demonstrated that it was far easier than had been supposed hitherto to mimic natural language dialogue on a computer. The user could type in sentences and would then see, either on a screen or a teletypewriter, plausible answers. A series of such inputs and their answers resembled a conversation in which the machine appeared to have understood the human.

Doctor

The program actually consisted of two elements: a general algorithm which identified phrase boundaries and carried out a limited range of grammatical transformations (such as replacing 'I' with 'you'), and a database which Weizenbaum called the script. The script consisted of a list of keywords which the program would look for when the user typed in a sentence, and a set of responses or response frames which would be printed out. Most of the responses were associated with particular keywords, but there were also some noncommittal responses, such as 'Please go on', which the program would print if it had not found any of its keywords. Weizenbaum drew an analogy between ELIZA and an actress, capable of conversation but with nothing to say until she had learned her lines (1976, p.3). The best known script, and the one which was most often used for demonstration, was DOCTOR, in which the computer takes over the role of the psychiatrist in an interview conducted according to the principles of the Carl Rogers school of psychotherapy. This was particularly appropriate, since it is characteristic of such interviews that the psychiatrist directs as little as possible and echoes the patient's words frequently.

The pathetic fallacy

Weizenbaum found three reactions to the program which disturbed him, two of which concern the present discussion. The first, perhaps less important, was the tendency to anthropomorphize and then to become emotionally involved with the program. He reports, for instance, how his secretary once asked him to leave the room because she wanted a private conversation with ELIZA. She clearly expected some kind of comfort and intimacy from the experience, in spite of the fact that she had been present while the program was being developed and therefore knew in outline how its effects were achieved (1976, p.6). There is, of course, a universal tendency for us to anthropomorphize and form emotional bonds with machines and tools, and to treat any unpredictability in their behaviour as if it showed will or understanding. This does not usually reach the level of delusional thinking, but, Weizenbaum writes:

> If [man's] reliance on such machines is to be based on something other than unmitigated despair or blind faith, he must explain to himself what these machines do and even how they do it. [. . .] Yet most men don't understand computers to even the slightest degree. So unless they are capable of very great skepticism (the kind we bring to bear while watching a stage magician), they can explain the computer's intellectual feats only by bringing to bear the single analogy available to them, that is their model of their own capacity to think. No wonder, then, that they overshoot the mark.
>
> (Weizenbaum 1976, pp. 9–10)

The magisterial fallacy

Even more disturbing, though, was a reaction that Weizenbaum encountered among some professional colleagues, namely that the DOCTOR script or a development of it up to some more powerful level could be used as a serious therapeutic aid, providing mechanized psychiatric interviewing at a price far below what a human interviewer would charge. This involved not only an overly optimistic view of the development of which ELIZA-type programs were capable, but a hideously pessimistic and mechanistic view of the human interviewer's role in therapy and counselling. If the machine could capture all the significant elements of the therapist's contribution, then the human therapist was capturable, i.e. was contributing nothing but the type of data processing which was understood and represented in the machine's program. The same fallacy (I hope it is a fallacy) underlies the efforts that have been made to create bigger and better teaching computers which will solve all educational problems with elaborations of tutorial dialogue, described as 'intelligent tutoring systems'.

The components of an intelligent machine tutor

To be characterized as intelligent an educational system needs five components. The first is a representation of the subject knowledge to be taught, about which O'Shea and Self say:

> The large majority of the thousands of computer-assisted learning programs in existence 'do not know what they are doing' when they teach. The idea of computers 'knowing' anything is a difficult one, but for the moment let us simply say that most programs do not know the subject under discussion in the sense of being able to answer unanticipated questions, and do not know enough about the individual student to be able to adapt the teaching session to his needs. If we want to build computer-assisted learning programs to answer unanticipated questions and to individualise teaching — and we assume we do — then we must try to make the necessary knowledge available to the computer.
>
> (O'Shea and Self 1983, pp. 3–4)

The second component, also touched on by O'Shea and Self, is a model of the learner, i.e. an account of strategies that learners may adopt in solving problems together with a means of storing the history of how the current learner has dealt with the problems so far presented. The third component is a means of self-adjustment; the machine, too, has to be able to 'learn from experience'. The fourth is a channel by which the machine can explain its own decisions and procedures in a way which corresponds to human ways of thinking; this is what Donald Michie describes as the 'human window' (Michie and Johnston 1984, p.71). The fifth, and in some ways the most important, is a language understanding system, or parser, so that the machine can make sense of the learner's inputs in natural language. Obviously there can be no 'unanticipated questions' if the machine has no grammar with which to understand them.

All of these components are gradually being developed, though only with considerable effort. The effort itself is worth making; as a result of the research, we are beginning to understand a little better how knowledge can be represented and stored, what learning strategies learners use, what kind of explanations they demand, and how language itself works. As I suggested in the introduction, we gain insights by using the computer as a mirror. But the product, the intelligent tutoring systems which are created by this work, are still feeble imitations of the human teacher. They are superior, certainly, in one respect: they do not forget things. But they are miserably deficient in three ways. In the first place they have no breadth of knowledge, no ability to find illuminating comparisons in the everyday experience shared by learner and teacher. Secondly, they are insensitive, with very few channels by which they can get messages from the learner. At the moment the available channels are the keyboard, pointing devices like light pens and mice, and embryonic voice recognition devices which do little more than identify words from a list. None of these provides ways of reading the learner's immediate feelings. The third of the computer's deficiencies is that it has no love or enthusiasm to share.

The customers

I do not know when, if ever, we will get mechanical teachers which can outperform human beings. However, there is no reason to wait for machines to become intelligent; like the shopkeeper in the story at the beginning of this chapter, the machines already have intelligent customers. A good deal of the effort devoted to intelligent tutoring systems seems to be based on what I call the 'magisterial fallacy', the belief that nothing is learned unless it is explicitly taught. Textbooks, machines and, all too often, human teachers tend to treat learners as ignorant idiots who need every problem solved for them. On the contrary, learning requires only a stimulating environment which provides feedback, one in which the laws of cause and effect work normally.

Role reversal

A computer which supplies such an environment can be treated as something to experiment with. One example would be a grammatical parser, i.e. a program which analyses sentences and shows how each word is functioning (its part of speech) and how the words are grouped into phrases and clauses. I have used simple devices of this kind with advanced learners (overseas students at a British university) purely as a means of getting them interested in grammar, but I am sure they could be used at lower levels. One program which uses a parser, DODOES by Muriel Higgins, asks the user to type in a statement, and then adds a question tag to it. If the input sentence is 'HE LOVES CREAM' it would print out 'HE LOVES CREAM, DOESN'T HE?' As it analyses the sentence, it may come back to the user with questions; for instance, if the input statement was 'BABY SWALLOWS FLY', it would ask 'IS SWALLOWS A NOUN OR A VERB?' If you answer 'VERB' it will then ask 'IS THE PRONOUN FOR BABY HE, SHE OR IT?' and then produce 'BABY SWALLOWS FLY, DOESN'T HE?' If, on the other hand, you had told it that SWALLOWS was a noun, it would produce 'BABY SWALLOWS FLY, DON'T THEY?' It has no recognition vocabulary apart from pronouns, auxiliary verbs and negative particles (NO, NOT, NEVER), so it depends on the answers it gets. The point about this is that learners can actually see the effects of different answers, and they can readily be prompted into trying out ambiguous sentences, and are keen to discuss the way the program works to get its effects. One by-product of the work is that learners make use of reference grammars to check the machine in doubtful cases.

This is a very different use of a parser from those foreseen by most designers of parsing utilities. When asked, they may tell you that their parsers can be used for essay correction. I believe it makes more sense to ask learners to correct what the machine does than vice versa, since in the process they are likely to learn a good deal about the under-lying grammatical realities and the rules which the machine is using. In ordinary classrooms opportunities for experiment may be limited; what the machine can do for us is to put the 'trial' back into trial-and-error.

The BOOH factor

Too much respect for the machine will inhibit this kind of experi-mental approach, but fortunately there is in most of us a very healthy counter-instinct, which leads us to want to insult the machine when it is being magisterial. We see this most clearly when the computer prompts us to type in our name. If we can perceive a proper reason for this, then we will enter the name accurately. Otherwise, particu-larly when we are playing with demonstration programs, most users will enter something playful, such as Brigitte Bardot, Adolf Hitler or Kiss-me-quick. Later we can relish being addressed as 'Adolf', particularly if the computer's messages sound patronizing or cosy. ELIZA in particular lends itself to this form of exploitation; one can enjoy oneself trying to enter the most grotesque exaggerations and watch the machine respond in a deadpan or pseudo-caring fashion. Or one can enter nonsense, and laugh as it reflects these inputs as if they made sense. One may learn a certain amount about ELIZA's language analyser in the process, which may in turn lead to obser-vations about the grammatical structure of language itself; used this way ELIZA can be an interesting piece of language-learning material. The instinct towards deliberate irreverence has been christened the BOOH factor by Muriel Higgins (1981), and there are numerous ways in which it can be harnessed to language-learning ends, some of which will be examined in later chapters.

Magisterial thinking and CLOZE procedure

The habit of thinking magisterially is difficult to shed, particularly among trained teachers. This became very apparent to me during a recent public discussion when Christopher Jones was demonstrating and describing his CLOZEMASTER, a program which creates cloze exercises out of texts in a very flexible way.

Cloze is now a very familiar technique with numerous variations of detail. Originally it was intended to measure the readability of text. A prose extract was printed with the first sentence intact but with words deleted at a fixed interval (usually six, seven or eight) thereafter. The passage was then given to a target group of readers. If they failed to restore thirty-eight per cent of the missing words, the book from which the passage was taken was judged too difficult. If they could restore more than fifty-three per cent, the book was thought to be one which the group could read independently. Between these figures, the book could be read with support from the teacher.

Cloze quickly moved on to being used as a testing technique, evaluating individual learners' performance rather than materials. Much of the appeal of the technique lies in the ease with which cloze tests can be constructed, but this was reinforced by experiments which showed that cloze scores correlated extremely well with tests of global ability. This is no doubt due to the fact that in order to restore arbitrarily deleted words the learner must call on a wide range of knowledge: sentence grammar, discourse connectedness, and common sense and general knowledge. However, the individual scoring immediately put into dispute the nature of a right answer. Should the marker accept only the original word, or an acceptable synonym? Several research projects showed that the practical difference between the two styles of marking was negligible, but some notion of fairness and authority has led many teachers to prefer the latter. Meanwhile varieties of cloze exercise proliferated. These included multiple-choice cloze; rational cloze, in which words of a given grammatical class would be deleted (bringing cloze much closer to discrete-point grammar testing); a form of cloze without gaps in which the location of the deleted words had to be identified as well as the words themselves; and CLOZENTROPY, an interesting variation first investigated by Darnell in 1968 and then developed at Moray House on a computer, in which all student answers are stored, and the individual's score for an item is based only on his or her closeness to the majority of answers, not on comparison with a nominally correct answer or a table of acceptable answers (Darnell 1968; Cousin 1983).

Computer CLOZE

A cloze exercise on a microcomputer makes an already easy process even easier; the machine can read in text from a disk or tape and can insert gaps at whatever interval is asked for, thus making different exercises from the same text. The gaps can be suppressed, shown in a standard form, or shown with dashes for each deleted letter, thus giving a clue to the length of the missing word. The exercise can be printed out for completion away from the machine, or tackled by a student at the screen and keyboard. In the latter case students can have more than one attempt at each answer, and can be offered help (e.g. word length or first letter) after a failure. The computer can process the texts so rapidly that many of the decisions, e.g. about the deletion interval, the kind of help wanted, or about the scoring, can be made by the students themselves; the machine will produce a tailor-made exercise to the student's specification within a few seconds. But the one thing that a small microcomputer cannot provide is assessment of the acceptability of alternative answers. There is not the storage space to equip the machine with the knowledge that *blonde* may replace *fair* if the next word is *hair* but not if the next word is *play*.

When I attended Christopher Jones's demonstration, I was astonished at the extent to which this shortcoming, if it is one, was resented by the teachers present at the demonstration. The machine was inadequate, they felt, if it could not give authoritative rulings on acceptability, if it appeared to mark a 'right' answer as 'wrong'. Many of them could not bring themselves to accept Jones's counter-argument that the machine's challenge did not involve notions of rightness or wrongness in language. The program was inviting the learner to restore a piece of written text which had been created by a particular writer on a particular occasion. The learner would win the game by guessing correctly what that writer had written, not by creating an acceptable piece of English with the same meaning. Indeed the effort of guessing often makes students aware of stylistic variation and paraphrases which they might not notice otherwise. None of this carried any weight with some members of the audience, who clearly expected the computer to mirror what they would have done in class, namely give an absolute judgement on each proposed answer.

STORYBOARD

I have encountered similar reactions from teachers who have seen or used my own STORYBOARD program, or variants of it such as

TELLTALE in the Longman QUARTEXT package. This is a development of CLOZE to its logical extreme, where every word of a text is deleted, leaving only indications of word length and punctuation, together with a title to indicate the general semantic area. The learners (this is usually a group task) have to enter words which they think might occur, either content words suggested by the title or function words, some of which are bound to be present. Each correctly guessed word is entered on screen in all the right locations, and the text is built up gradually in jigsaw fashion. The puzzle is challenging and engrossing, and much lively discussion is generated.

A common question from teachers, however, is 'What happens when a learner puts in a spelling mistake?' The answer is that the machine obeys its instructions. It hunts for, say, the word FREIND and reports that it failed to find it. It has no means of knowing that the learner should have typed in FRIEND. There are some teachers who find this unacceptable. A machine which fails to administer a metaphorical rap over the knuckles when a language error occurs is one they see no point in using.

Spelling

The topic of spelling is one which has strong magisterial overtones, particularly for English. This is due to the arbitrariness of some of our spelling conventions and the difficulty of deriving the correct spelling of a word purely from sound clues. The teacher and the dictionary, therefore, have great authority, and, apart from a few derivation rules, teachers offer few learning procedures other than memorization. One of the hangovers from the behaviourist era is a fear of mistakes, since behaviourist theory maintained that correct behaviour had to be reinforced and any uncorrected error would be a counter-reinforcement.

Another program of mine, called PRINTER'S DEVIL, takes a set of words assumed to be familiar (e.g. the vocabulary of a coursebook) and systematically mutilates them. The learner's task is to identify the principle behind the mutilation. Given the words FARMER, APPLE, LOVING, BEFORE and YELLOW, the program might print each word backwards:

REMRAF
ELPPA
GNIVOL
EROFEB
WOLLEY

or it might switch the first and last letters:

RARMEF
EPPLA
GOVINL
EEFORB
WELLOY

or it might remove all the vowels:

FRMR
PPL
LVNG
BFR
YLLW

At more advanced levels the rules may be applied conditionally; the word is left unmutilated unless it has, say, an even number of letters, or ends in a vowel, or begins with a letter in the first half of the alphabet. The activity is closely related to a more generalized game known as Kolodny's Game or 'Find the Rule'. The process one asks the learners to go through is:

1. recognize some of the words in their mutilated forms;
2. work out a process for restoring the correct form from the mutilated form;
3. apply this process to other mutilated forms to see if it yields familiar words;
4. test the hypothesis on sufficient further examples to confirm or refute it.

The activity is fun, and its educational value may be as much in the thinking and discussion it generates as in any direct learning from the program.

Whenever I use or demonstrate this program, however, I can be sure that some teachers will be indignant at me for showing spelling mistakes on screen, thus encouraging students to learn and remember the mutilated forms. The computer seems to have inherited some of the respect that many of us still feel for print, expecting everything in print to be correct and true. Here again is a symptom of our giving the machine a magisterial role, and of crediting learners with too little common sense.

Exploratory programs

Perhaps the area of greatest misunderstanding is that of exploratory programs, to use the term coined by Johns (1982). These are typically very short programs which will execute a morphological change, e.g. add a third-person or plural S-ending or an ING-ending to an input word, or select A or AN in front of a noun or noun phrase. The DODOES program discussed on page 20 is another example of an exploratory program. They embody a minute fragment of a grammar, a small set of rules. The learners' task is to explore the adequacy of the program by giving it a variety of inputs; ultimately they are trying to find the exceptional cases that the program cannot handle, to force the program to make a mistake.

The machine's role is obviously non-magisterial, since it is responding to any input in any order and makes no evaluation. What worries teachers is the magisterial vacuum. In the A/AN program, for instance, if a student enters FURNITURE, the machine will respond A FURNITURE, meaning, roughly, given that there is a count noun FURNITURE, the correct form of article to use with it is A. The machine makes no judgement about whether FURNITURE is a count noun. Indeed it will respond just as readily to nonsense words as to English words, and much can be learned about the underlying algorithm by feeding it with nonsense.

So, if the magister does not reside in the machine, where can he be found? Who can prevent the activity from becoming a chaos of uncertainty? One obvious answer is a hovering human teacher supervising the group's activity and intervening when necessary. Another answer is the collective knowledge of the group, who, unless the activity is wildly wrong for their level, will usually make a relevant ruling or summon the teacher in cases of doubt. A third answer is reference books, and one merit of exploratory programs is that they often drive learners to reference books in the search for exceptional cases which the program may not be able to handle. A fourth answer is the dormant knowledge of the individual; given time to remember and an unthreatening atmosphere in which to think, learners can quite often answer their own questions.

Intervention

Intervention, however, is always magisterial. It is an initiative: player A is doing something which player B has not asked him to. Even a magister's presence can amount to tacit intervention. The magister's silence is then an assurance to the learner that no major error has yet occurred. Sometimes this is reassuring and valuable. At other times it can destroy the whole point of an activity.

On several occasions I have used computer programs with learners or demonstrated them to teachers and have been overtaken by a power cut or mechanical failure. When this happens I continue by pretending to be the computer. I ask for inputs and respond exactly as the computer would. Since in many cases I have written the algorithms myself, I know them well enough to do this. I have found, though, that the activity begins to liven up only when my class or audience become sure that I will offer no help other than what the computer would have given. Until they can treat me like the machine, they will not join in the activity with zest.

Mario Rinvolucri has designed class activities derived from computer programs written by me or my colleague Tim Johns (Rinvolucri 1985). These include: a simplified form of the STORYBOARD program described above; a version of a program called PINPOINT in which the title of a text has to be guessed from a minute fragment of the text itself; and variations on the exploratory programs A/AN and S-ENDING. Rinvolucri reported to me that teachers who use these activities have found that they do not work well while the teacher is facing the class. Eye contact, smiles and frowns, normally so valuable in most forms of teaching, seem to inhibit guesswork and suppress experiment; the class expect guidance and take it from the facial messages. The solution has been for teachers to turn their backs on the class, so that their responses become impersonal.

The teacher facing the class is a magister, and what he does is in some sense to play God, loving, knowing, guiding, and judging. The teacher with his back to the class, the pedagogue, is playing Nature, impersonal, governed by laws of cause and effect, sometimes appearing cruel, mysterious or stupid. The natural role for the computer is the latter. To exploit pedagogue or computer in order to learn requires a willingness to initiate and a readiness to experiment, and this may entail changes of attitude on the part of the learner. Formal education trains learners to become responders, answering questions but rarely asking them. It may require guidance from a magister to begin the process of de-training, so that exploratory learning can begin again. This is the subject of the following chapters.

2 The language

'*Par ma foi! il y a plus de quarante ans que je dis de la prose sans que j'en susse rien.*'
(Good heavens! I've been speaking prose for more than forty years without knowing it.)

Molière, *Le Bourgeois Gentilhomme*

Using our first language in daily life, we can go for days, months, or even years without giving any conscious thought to the medium we are using. We carry out prodigious amounts of talking, listening and reading and only occasionally think about the ways that meanings are expressed, the oddity of certain idioms, or the variety of styles available to us. Only when we write are we likely to give more attention to language forms; we may need to recast a sentence if it does not read well, and most of us, especially if English is the language we write, have to pay some attention to the spelling system. Generally, however, we give as little thought to language while we are using it as we do to air while we are breathing it.

Foreign-language learners, in contrast, think about the language almost all the time. They struggle to remember words; they rehearse tables of word endings in their minds in an attempt to get the grammar right; they worry about pronunciation. If what they are doing is going through practice exercises or drills, then they give almost no thought to meaning, since there is no need to bother. In conversation they are not unconcerned with meaning, but may, if the encoding task is particularly difficult, forget meaning momentarily and utter something ludicrous. I have several times heard stories of people visiting a country whose language they are learning at an elementary level. Approached by a stranger and asked for directions, say, to the post office, they laboriously produce the textbook answer, '*Vous prenez la deuxième rue à gauche.*' Only later does it strike them that they have no idea where the post office really is.

Aims of language learning

The aim of virtually all language courses must be to help learners move from the condition of struggling awareness of the medium towards that of confident and unconscious use. Courses differ in how and when they seek to achieve this. A structural course would see the switch occurring fairly late, after learners have acquired enough resources to cope with many different language applications. A communicative course would try to make the switch early but limit it to a few language applications ('notions' or 'functions'), adding further applications later.

There are many people, following both kinds of course, who fail to learn languages. They leave school or give up their classes while they are still at the struggling stage and have no mental energy to spare for the task of thinking about meaning. Their reward from the effort they have put in is negligible, and they may have acquired the conviction that language learning is impossible for them. Yet languages are quite clearly learnable: the evidence for that is the fact that we all learn at least one, while some of us learn more than one extremely well. Learning our first language is by no means quick or easy, but success is virtually universal, and the degree of skill we achieve is remarkably uniform. Of course there are people who use language more effectively, more colourfully, or more flexibly than others, but every native speaker of a language seems to be equipped with a sure command of a grammatical system and of a vocabulary adequate to their life style. Variability among speakers is far more evident in the degree to which they are aware of what they are doing or can analyse language than in the basic skill of using it.

Command

One interesting metaphor which is deeply embedded in the language which we use to talk about education is that of 'command'. We talk about commanding a skill or a musical instrument or a foreign language, and yet we hardly ever discuss just what this term implies. Like the schoolmaster's 'insolence', it is something we cannot define but always recognize. We occasionally use the near synonym 'mastery', especially in the USA, and often distinguish 'mastery', which is the skill achieved, from 'mastering', which is the process of achieving it. The metaphor recalls, perhaps, the training of circus animals. When we command a skill, it is dormant until we crack the whip. Then it arises obediently to perform its tricks for us.

Memory and connectedness

How, then, is command achieved? Obviously memory is one element;

we cannot use a language unless we can remember the words for many common concepts. Since the relationship between the forms of words and their meanings is arbitrary, there seems to be no alternative to memory as a means of mastering vocabulary. We could not deduce that the French for 'dog' is *chien*; somebody or something would have to tell us. Memory, however, does not have to come from deliberate acts of memorization. For instance, many of us know a dozen or more telephone numbers of people we call frequently; we never set out to learn those numbers, but simply discovered after a while that we no longer needed to look them up. A good deal of knowledge of a foreign language is of this I-have-been-here-before kind. The trouble is that what has been unconsciously remembered is liable to be forgotten as soon as it goes out of regular use, and that it may not be available to the conscious mind outside the context in which it is normally used. Recently somebody asked me which key on a computer keyboard usually contains the apostrophe. If I had had a computer in front of me my fingers could have moved to the key in about a quarter of a second, but I needed nearly ten seconds to think of and express the answer in words.

Pronunciation

It is also clear that we do not learn pronunciation from deliberate acts of memorization but rather by unconscious assimilation of our exposure to speech. Teachers, of course, do try to teach pronunciation by correcting errors and giving drills on particular sounds and features of rhythm. Many of us have to admit that the payoff from these activities is minute; the errors creep back almost immediately, and the students still do not sound English when they speak English. Yet many of them can produce English sounds when they sing and, if asked to mimic rather than repeat, are capable of accurately reproducing an English accent. There is a strong emotional component in the use of foreign sounds, but the underlying learning seems to be taking place anyway, waiting to be released as soon as the learner wants to identify with the foreign speech community.

Grammar

Other aspects of language, in particular the ability to put words together grammatically, seem to involve not memory but the active re-processing of what is in one's memory. We do not just remember rules of grammar, but rather we use them creatively, to understand

and produce novel utterances. In the early stages of learning, while the components of grammar are still being memorized, you notice grammar principally as an obstacle to communication. Either you are continually being interrupted as the teacher corrects your errors, or else you feel tongue-tied because you are not sure what ending to use or how to put a sentence together. The grammar of a highly inflected language can seem like a barbed wire fence all round you; every time you flex your linguistic muscles you get scratched. It is only much later that you find yourself using grammar as a way of enlarging your repertoire of messages and of finding paraphrases for the meanings you want to express. Grammar then turns into a means of releasing the language rather than confining it.

This is not to deny that there is sometimes great arbitrariness in grammar. There is no logical reason why in standard English we say 'himself' rather than 'hisself', or cannot say 'I enjoy to go to the seaside' or 'I wish seeing you soon.' In fact there is a formal similarity between language and games, in that the rules define the activity. If you play a game of chess in which it is legal to make the castling move when your king is in check, then you are not playing chess. These may be your house rules and the game, played this way in your own circle, may be just as good a game as the standard form of chess, but it is still a different game. In the same way the rules of English grammar define what is or is not a 'legal move' of English. While seeming to place a restriction on all the things you might want to do, they actually create the possibilities for communication. Grammar is the means by which one can match the infinity of possible messages to a set of legal utterances which can be understood by another user of the same language. Although some of the arbitrary cases can only be learned from tuition or experience, i.e. they cannot be deduced, what is generally remarkable about grammar is how much we get for how little.

Coherence

Subjects that we learn from some kind of organized study, rather than just picking them up from experience, divide broadly into those which form a coherent system, such as the theory of electrical circuits or the game of bridge, and those in which the component facts are less connected, such as key dates in history or the numbers used in an office filing system. In the former case learning may be slow, but it should reach a point where one sees the 'connectedness' of the system; having reached this watershed it is usually quite hard to forget what one has learned, and one may well feel a sense of 'command'. In the case of disconnected facts, forgetting is related directly to the passage of time. A related case is that of a tactile skill, such as playing a musical instrument, in which command must be maintained by regular practice.

Language seems to fall between these extremes, though tending towards the second. The relationship of word to meaning (or of word to grammatical gender, say, in languages like German or Swahili) is arbitrary, and so there is inevitably much in language which has to be learned unsystematically and which can be forgotten. This applies to native speakers as much as to foreign learners: we can forget technical terms that we no longer use just as easily as we forget the names of former acquaintances. The grammatical system, in contrast, seems to form the kind of connected system which is much harder to forget once mastered.

The watershed effect

Some evidence for this can be provided by a phenomenon which I call the 'watershed effect', one I know from personal and reported experience but which I have never seen described in the professional literature. It is the ability to recall to the day, virtually to the hour, the time when one switched from being a struggling learner of a language to being in control of it, from laborious mental translation to a fairly spontaneous ability to encode messages. In my own case I have had one such experience out of four languages which I have learned to a reasonably advanced standard, but I have spoken to a number of Peace Corps volunteers who reported similar Eureka-like moments. The typical conditions for such an experience seem to be several months of classroom tuition followed by a period of immersion in the target language environment, which is the normal pattern of Peace Corps training. The watershed may be reached in a few weeks or only after many months. In the majority of cases it is never perceived: mastery, if it comes at all, creeps up on the learner unawares.

The great unknown

In his book *Programmed learning and the language teacher*, published in 1969, A P R Howatt presents a sample of programmed learning and asks the reader to work through it. The sample is only four pages long and contains twelve frames, using Skinnerian linear programming. The subject matter is comparative adjectives in English; 'He is older than his wife.' The author then gives a questionnaire to invite introspection about the experience, and follows this with some discussion of each question. The most interesting of the question/discussion pairs are the following:

15. After the pupil has worked through the programme would you, in general, expect him to be able
    a) to use the pattern in conversation?
    b) to recognize and understand it in someone else's speech?
    c) to use the pattern correctly in writing?
    d) to recognize it in reading?
    e) none of these?

16. Suppose the programme had been worked through orally in class or in the language laboratory, would you then expect the pupil to be able to employ the pattern correctly in spontaneous conversation?

Discussion

15. (d), and possibly (b). This is of course a highly complex question and depends on what is understood by *expect*. You could not, it seems to me, *expect* the pupils to use the pattern spontaneously either in speech or in writing because they have not been asked to do so in the programme. However they have been asked to construct sentences more or less unaided in accordance with the rule underlying the pattern. This is the most that a controlled teaching technique can do. The next step, the successful use of the rule in an appropriate situation, is the 'great unknown' of language teaching, . . .
16. No. This is a continuation of the previous argument. There is no fundamental distinction between doing exercises of this controlled kind in speech or in writing when it comes to the *spontaneous* production of language. Again, the pupil may make the transition for himself but you cannot *expect* him to do so. Discussions on language teaching sometimes imply that if the pupil is actively engaged in producing comprehensible foreign speech, then he is learning how to speak the foreign language. This is not a logical deduction at all, . . .

(Howatt 1969, pp. 9, 11–12)

Howatt's phrase 'the great unknown' is the most honest admission I have seen in print of our ignorance of the learning process. We simply do not know how facts, experience and rules are processed and internalized. This does not apply just to language learning; it is as much a mystery why telephone numbers or pieces of 'general knowledge' (the kind that features in quiz games) are sometimes absorbed with little conscious effort and sometimes not recalled even after many exposures and much memorization. There is variation between learners, some finding it easier than others. There is also great variation within a single person about what is retained. We all, I expect, have an abundance of 'useless facts' that will spring to mind in conversation or if we participate in a quiz game. But there are also many thousands more which will not, which either stay on the tip of the tongue or are totally forgotten, and yet there is no apparent reason why the first set should have been absorbed and not the second.

Motivation

Diversity of achievement among a group of learners sometimes baffles teachers; they can find no explanation for uneven performance in the way they have taught. After all, a group of infants within a speech community, given a great variety of exposure to their first language, somehow manage to acquire a fairly uniform (and high) level of command. Why is it, then, that a reasonably homogeneous group of classroom learners, who have had virtually identical exposure to and practice of a foreign language, contrive to exhibit a huge variety of levels of performance? The standard explanation is *motivation*.

Carrot and stick

The traditional view of motivation is to equate human motivation with that of the donkey, desire for the carrot or fear of the stick; low motivation implies lack of interest or laziness. Such a view, of course, treats the learner as essentially unwilling to learn and needing to be set moving by some external pressure. It clearly does not fit the many kinds of 'self-motivated' learners, notably all pre-school children and a good many adult learners. To account for those cases some writers distinguish two kinds of motivation, *integrative* and *instrumental*. Integrative motivation is an emotional desire to master language because one admires and wants to identify with the target culture. Instrumental motivation is the desire to learn because one needs to speak the language (or pass an exam which certifies that you can speak it) in order to succeed in one's job or gain promotion. The second of these is more or less the carrot and stick re-stated as a 'need' for the skill. Supporters of a carrot-and-stick model of motivation can point to the success of courses like those in Russian and Chinese run by the British Army at Crail. The national servicemen on these courses had a relatively privileged life with fewer parades and lighter discipline than the majority of soldiers. They knew, however, that if they failed a Saturday test they would be sent back to basic training on the

Monday. (For a full discussion of motivation, see Ellis 1985, especially pp. 116–119.)

The affective filter

Newer orthodoxies have paid more attention to anxiety as a factor in language learning, not the soldier's anxiety about failing the test but the learners' anxiety about making fools of themselves with their ignorance or mistakes. If one student has learned less than another, it must be because he or she is less open to language inputs or, in more fashionable phraseology, has erected an 'affective filter' (see, e.g. Krashen 1982). The affective filter hypothesis seems to be the only component of Krashen's language acquisition theory which provides any explanation for differences in achievement; as such it is a very convenient fallback.

Measuring learning

Before one can explain diversity, however, one needs to know whether it exists, and this is more problematic than it sounds. In a behaviourist view of learning, teaching is conditioning, i.e. securing a change of behaviour. The learner behaves one way before the lesson and another way after it; the efficiency of learning can be measured by comparing the behaviour before and after. A cognitive view, however, would be that learning relates to mental 'maps' of the world which we draw in our heads. We assimilate experience, and must modify the maps if the experience does not fit what we already know. Overt behaviour changes may be one sign of such learning, but we cannot be sure that the absence of a behavioural change means that there has been no learning, nor that a change of behaviour implies that the desired learning has taken place. These are issues which I shall return to in Chapter 6. Meanwhile, although we can be fairly sure that there is a great deal of diversity among learners and within each learner, we do not have evidence of exactly how one learner differs from another, since no learner's mental map is available for study.

Suppressing learning

What we can be fairly sure of is that the learning instinct is naturally strong: we are always trying to make sense of our environment. Learning will occur, both with children and adults, unless it is in some way suppressed. The commonest conditions for this to happen are when everything in the environment is too complex and unfamiliar to be put in order, or when everything in the environment is too familiar and offers no challenge. The first we would describe as 'too difficult' and the second as 'too easy'. Both sets of circumstances produce the condition known as boredom, the switching off of the learning instinct. Thus, although the causes are quite different, the symptoms may look very similar.

Caretaker speech

For language learners it is very easy to create an environment in which the material is too difficult to assimilate: just expose them to unsimplified speech before they have any familiarity with simpler comprehensible messages. Many hours of having my car radio on in Egypt and of listening to official speeches in Yugoslavia have made very little dent in my ignorance of Arabic and Serbo-Croatian. I did not get enough of what Krashen calls 'caretaker speech', which might have permitted me to build some conceptual structures by using intelligent guesswork about the meanings. Language, particularly spoken language, is an especially problematic subject for mental model building since it does not 'stand still' to be examined; if one cannot decode speech at the same pace that a speaker is speaking, the auditory traces are of very little use. The learner needs to spend time in a protected environment where somebody, through slowing down, simplifying, or repeating, supplies material which can be assimilated before the memory traces get overlaid with new confusing signals.

If the environment is over-protected, however, and in particular if the exposure is reduced to unchallenging forms which require no 'solution', such as vocabulary lists, then there is a danger of the second condition occurring. The material is felt to be too easy and hence irrelevant. It may still not be mastered, since the kind of memory activity involved is very vulnerable to decay.

Rough-tuning

Finding the kind of material which will keep the learning instinct stimulated for any individual is a considerable problem for any teacher. Finding material which will keep a class of learners simultaneously engaged may seem like an impossible one. Stephen Krashen claims that by 'rough-tuning' the language that a class is exposed to one can provide enough input at the critical level for all the learners to have their cognitive processes fed for at least a part of the time.

Even if this is true, it still sounds potentially wasteful. Is there a better way?

The language jigsaw puzzle

One can draw an analogy with the process of solving a jigsaw puzzle. The hundreds of separate pieces of the picture come out of the box in a random way, and the solver has to order them to turn them into something sensible. The strategy adopted by virtually everyone who attempts the task is to begin by looking for edges and corners, i.e. with pieces which can be recognized by their shape independently of what is drawn on them. This, one might say, corresponds to starting a language course with some basic sentence patterns and simple grammar. The next step is usually to work on parts of the picture which show relatively complex but familiar images, such as people, buildings, or ships. In the same way language learners add necessary situations and functions which take them away from the simple grammatical forms they began with. The jigsaw puzzler usually leaves to last the larger tracts of space, such as water and sky, in which the individual pieces convey less information. Here there is no precise analogy with language learning, except perhaps the general observation that languages are not easier at advanced levels.

One can be fairly sure that nobody would take up jigsaw puzzles if the only permitted way to solve them were to place each piece irrevocably as soon as it was drawn randomly out of the box. This would make the task 'too difficult' just as unsimplified speech is too difficult for the beginner at a language. Neither would there be much pleasure if each piece was sequentially numbered and the task consisted only of sorting them into numerical order. Here we have a counterpart of a drill approach which is 'too easy'. Each solver seeks an optimal challenge, neither too difficult nor too easy, and so do learners.

If we rely on teachers to select and devise optimal challenges for all the learners in their charge, we are certainly straining the teachers' powers of judgement to the limit and may well be demanding the impossible. The only alternative is to allow learners to find their own challenges by an exploration process. This is hardly possible in a pattern of mass education under a magisterial teacher, but the computer has made it feasible. In the next chapter I shall be looking at a number of ways in which an exploratory approach can be engendered and encouraged in the context of computer-assisted language learning.

Motivation or demotivation?

In virtually all accounts of computer-assisted learning projects increases in motivation are reported. Students seem to enjoy themselves more and are willing to spend more time at the keyboard than on more conventional activities. This phenomenon is not always welcomed: there is anxiety about the 'hypnotic' effect of the computer screen and the dangers of 'addiction'. It seems to me, though, that students enjoy computer work and spend time on it precisely because the computer readily provides optimal challenges. In view of this, it may be wrong to talk about the computer supplying motivation. The motivation is present all the time. Instead it is the exigencies of mass teaching that are supplying demotivation. Looked at in this way, many issues in the motivation debate become much easier to grasp. The task is not to enhance motivation, merely to reduce demotivation to the point where learners can set about finding their optimal challenges. (This would include providing ready help and answers to questions without any threats or implied criticism of the learner for needing to ask the question at all.) The optimal challenges supply experience, and the learners' cognitive processes draw the mental maps which turn experience into command. The lack of optimal challenges in mass instruction is a plausible explanation for the failure of most children to learn languages well at school.

3 The learner

Where there is much desire to learn, there of necessity will be much arguing, much writing, many opinions.

Milton, *Areopagitica*

There is an obvious sense in which learners are more important than teachers. Just as one cannot sell until there are people able and willing to buy, so one cannot teach unless there are people prepared to learn. The learners are the customers, whether or not they are paying for the product. Learners may learn without teachers, but teachers cannot teach without learners.

But it is equally obvious that learners do not usually learn well without teachers. Teachers who have experimented with very unstructured work often report that the learners are bewildered by it and waste their time; they do not necessarily find optimal challenges in free activity. Given opportunities to learn, in a library for instance, most of us will not find it as easy to cope with new subject matter as we would in a formal class. What this amounts to is that if you teach yourself you have to be both teacher and learner, and that is too hard a task for most of us to handle.

Learning paradigms

In 1977 a team led by Stephen Kemmis at the University of Norwich published an evaluation study of computers in education called 'How do students learn?' Kemmis and his colleagues identified four learning paradigms; in other words they classified computer-assisted lesson forms into four major types, distinguished from each other by unstated but implicit theoretical assumptions about how learning and teaching take place. The names they gave to the four paradigms were instructional, revelatory, conjectural, and emancipatory. The same terms can be used to describe more conventional lesson forms, although this particular scheme of classification would probably not have been adopted by anyone not working with computers. A highly encapsulated account of them from a teacher's point of view might be as follows:

Instructional: make statements and check for recall, as in standard forms of instruction and in programmed learning.
Revelatory: provide structured experience, as for instance in a simulation, and check for assimilation.
Conjectural: set tasks which allow students to cast around fairly freely for a solution, provide facilities, and hope that insights occur.
Emancipatory: provide the learner with tools to facilitate relevant learning activity ('authentic labour') and reduce irrelevant activity ('inauthentic labour').

Each of Kemmis's paradigms can be matched to a role for the learner, namely absorber, experiencer, explorer, and practitioner. The first of these requires a teacher, in fact a magister (though the magister may take the form of a highly structured 'teach-yourself' textbook or a piece of programmed learning). The second does not require a teacher at the execution stage, although a magister will probably set up, manage, and evaluate the experience. The third requires a pedagogue, a responsive teacher or an environment which is rich in feedback. The fourth requires no teacher other than a trainer to make sure the tools can be properly used.

Probably all four roles are adopted in turn in any extended piece of learning. The interesting question to ask is which roles assume prominence for different stages of learning and different types of subject matter. The first two roles are well understood by teachers, since we observe them from our magisterial side of the desk. The third role is less well understood, since we often do not see it at all, while the fourth is often ignored since it hardly seems to count as teaching or learning.

The work ethic

The fourth paradigm has a slightly different status from the others; the learner is a user of 'tools', such as books or pens, in many different contexts, and therefore the role of practitioner overlaps with the other roles. Kemmis uses the word emancipatory in connection with the computer's use as a tool precisely because it can free the learner from unnecessary work, what he calls inauthentic labour, and thereby increase relevant work opportunities. I came across an illustration of the difference between authentic and inauthentic labour a few years ago when I heard on radio the winner of a TV general knowledge quiz being asked to explain his success. He told the interviewer that he kept a set of encyclopedias in every room so that he never had to walk more than a few steps to find the answer to a question. Using the encyclopedias is authentic but walking to fetch them is inauthentic. When answers are easy to get, you ask more questions, especially when no loss of face is involved.

It is worth noting, however, how easy it is to invoke a work ethic to justify the inadequacy of tools. Copying texts from the blackboard into a notebook, rather than have them photocopied or duplicated, is sometimes described as 'useful language practice', even though it corresponds to no real-life use of language. (It may, of course, be a necessary makeshift if the school cannot afford any other way of putting texts in front of students.) If a school cannot afford to put a dictionary in each classroom, one is tempted to say, 'Well, it will force students to use the library.' What it actually forces them to do is use the dictionary much less than they might. Making learning difficult does not make it more valuable. Making learning convenient does, in general, increase the amount of it that takes place.

Word-processing

The value of emancipatory activities is shown most clearly by word-processing. Where there are self-access systems used by large numbers of students, it is usually the word-processing software which is the most popular. Since the installations are still all fairly recent and in schools which are privileged in terms of staff and resources, it may be dangerous to generalize too much. There is usually an enthusiastic staff member who takes trouble to give new students initial training in the use of the software and in editing techniques, and without this kind of support there might be far less usage. However, reports coming out of these schools suggest that learners are writing with greater enthusiasm and are far readier to correct and edit their work than they are when using only pen and paper, and this is surely to be welcomed. It seems, for instance, that when your work is displayed neatly, whether on screen or on paper, it becomes easier to read it as if you were an outsider, to judge the impression it will make on the target reader. This makes learners readier to return to what they have written and recast it.

Learners are often reluctant to make a start with word-processing if they have never used a typewriter before; the keyboard with its strange arrangement of letters seems frighteningly difficult to master. I have found the best way over this barrier is to start rather magisterially with worksheets assignments. I prepare a document on disk in the form of a short personal letter with all the personal details missing. Learners follow point-by-point instructions to load this document, scroll through it, insert personal names and place names, finish some sentences and delete others, and then save it and print it. The satisfaction of seeing a finished product which they can post to their family usually gets them wanting to do more, even if their typing skills are still at the hunt-and-peck stage. Real keyboard facility will come with practice once they have overcome their emotional resistance to the medium.

A word-processor also makes convenient the kind of collaborative writing project that writers like Bright and McGregor were recommending twenty years ago (Bright and McGregor 1970), with learners not only dividing up the sections of a topic that each would write about but also sharing responsibility for the appearance of the finished copy. A draft can be passed several times between a 'writer' and an 'editor', or circulated round a circle of editors before being adopted. A program called DEADLINE has been developed by the British Council for this purpose; it simulates the production of a local guidebook or information leaflet which has to be written from 'newsflashes' and tabular information available to the team of writers and editors. This kind of work increases the attention given, both by teachers and learners, to the process of writing rather than just the product.

Concordances

Another application of emancipatory learning has been in the use of concordances, in particular by Tim Johns with his MICRO-CONCORD program. Concordances are usually thought of as tools for the literary scholar or linguistic researcher. In computer form they allow you to search through a stored text for a particular word, and then see all the occurrences of that word printed out in a context, usually one complete line of eighty characters with the key word centred. A common word, like *the*, might produce several hundred citations per ten thousand words of text, but most content words would produce only a few, if any. For this reason concordance programs have mostly been used with vast stores of text, containing perhaps millions of words.

Johns, although not the first person to suggest in print that concordances could be used by learners, was able to miniaturize the whole concept by putting a concordance package into a small domestic computer (the Sinclair Spectrum) with a cheap storage device (the microdrive). This could be kept permanently available in the classroom and became, for some of his ESP students, almost as normal a tool as the dictionary. The stored texts were from the professional litera- ture that those students would be using so that, even if the sample was small (about 14,000 words in the project he describes), it was relevant. Whenever a question arose on, for instance, the use of a preposition or on the difference between a pair of near synonyms, the machine could produce a printout, and this in turn might lead to follow-up questions and further printout. (This follow-up activity could not easily be predicted or controlled, so that a teacher who was determined to follow a planned lesson might find the machine a liability.) Errors in written work could be dealt with by getting a print- out of the words which had been misused, so that learners made a direct comparison between their own usage and authentic text. Johns describes several other ways in which he used the concordance, and teachers in other circumstances and with different needs could no doubt find more (Johns 1986).

Obviously the work that Johns's students were doing was more than just looking up facts. Having obtained the printout they then looked at the citations and attempted to make sense of them. Some of the facts might spring to the eye very readily; for instance a set of citations for the word *same* is almost bound to show the word *the* in front of each occurrence. Others would require a good deal of counting and comparing; in effect the learners were discovering some of the facts of grammar. They were not just using tools; they were exploring the language, i.e. using conjectural learning.

Grammar

Learning the grammar of a foreign language is probably an area which always requires a blend of instructional, revelatory and conjectural approaches, although it does not always get them. The modern teacher is likely to introduce a new point of grammar indirectly by presenting a piece of text in which the new form occurs. Learners are expected to notice the form and deduce what it means before going on to a controlled practice stage in which they manipulate it and try to make it automatic. Later, when they make mistakes during free writing or conversation, the teacher can point out the mistakes, remind them of the context in which they first met the form, or bring back some of the practice drills.

In effect the teacher is starting with a revelatory approach and then switching to an instructional one. The conjectural approach is not part of the planned curriculum; if it happens at all, it will be in the course of reading and listening. Observed errors bring a reversion to the instructional approach. What is shown by the work that Johns and others have been doing is that this may be the wrong way round. While an instructional approach applied in a magisterial fashion may well be the best way to introduce what is totally new, a conjectural approach may be much more relevant to problems which are half known or half understood. Some further evidence for this comes from an article by Farrington in which he describes a conventional magisterial exercise on gender in French nouns: learners were shown a noun and had to supply *ce*, *cet* or *cette*. What Farrington's students (all of intermediate level or higher) reported was that the program was in some cases decreasing their confidence rather than increasing it; the conscious attention they were giving to choosing the right form seemed to be at the cost of whatever unconscious processes they otherwise used. A better approach might have been to let the learners speculate on how the native speaker of French assigns gender, and let the computer be a test bed for trying out hypotheses (Farrington 1986).

Exploratory programs

The actual mechanics of doing this are demonstrated by the exploratory programs already described in Chapter 1 (p. 26). The machine is programmed with a rule or rules for handling some feature of grammar, such as a word inflexion, a sentence transformation, or even the selection of an appropriate stylistic form. Learners input phrases into the machine in order to see what it does. They are trying to deduce the rules and assess their adequacy. In the case of Farrington's gender task, for instance, the machine would not be given any word lists but would have some kind of decision procedure for assigning the likely gender on the basis of word shapes. Learners would feed it with words and check the machine's choice against the dictionary if necessary. In this particular case it is easy to resolve any uncertainty; if one also fed the machine nonsense words to test its rules, then one might also need to consult native speakers to see what gender they would assign. Notice that when you use a computer in this way, each student is not learning from the computer but from the total learning environment, an environment that includes reference books, native speakers or expert speakers (of whom the teacher is the most accessible), the pooled knowledge of the group, and the dormant knowledge of the individual. The computer is not sealing the learner off in a private dialogue where all the answers and all the certainty must come from the screen.

JACKASS

The whole exploratory principle can be very well illustrated by a classic computer activity, originally known as ANIMAL. Other versions have been published as PANGOLIN and TREE OF KNOWLEDGE, and I have written an extended version under the title JACKASS. The basis is that the user thinks of an object and the computer will try to guess what it is. In my version the starting categories are Animals, Objects, Cities or People. (In other forms of the program, such as Acornsoft's TREE OF KNOWLEDGE, the user can create new categories.)

Let us suppose that the user chooses Animals. A session of play might go like this.

DOES YOUR ANIMAL LIVE ON A FARM?

YES.

I KNOW.   IT'S A COW.   IS THAT RIGHT?

NO.

YOU KNOW MORE THAN I DO.   PLEASE TELL ME THE NAME OF YOUR ANIMAL.

HORSE.

THANK YOU.   NOW PLEASE GIVE ME A QUESTION BEGIN-NING 'DOES IT' TO DISTINGUISH A HORSE FROM A COW.

DOES IT RUN RACES?

FOR A HORSE WHAT IS THE ANSWER?

YES.

THANK YOU.   NOW I KNOW 3 DIFFERENT ANIMALS. SHALL WE PLAY AGAIN?

YES.

THINK OF AN ANIMAL.   DOES YOUR ANIMAL LIVE ON A FARM?

YES.

DOES IT RUN RACES?

NO.

I KNOW.   IT'S A COW.   IS THAT RIGHT?

NO.

YOU KNOW MORE THAN I DO. PLEASE TELL ME THE
NAME OF YOUR ANIMAL.

PIG.

and so on.

The machine is given one starting question, DOES YOUR
ANIMAL LIVE ON A FARM?, and two animals, COW and
ELEPHANT. This is the sum of its knowledge of the universe;
anything which is not a cow is an elephant, and anything which is
not an elephant is a cow. It is up to the user to teach it, by means
of the guessing game, that the universe contains other animals. Every
time the machine 'guesses' wrong, it adds the new animal and the new
Yes/No question to its database, and appears to become 'cleverer'.

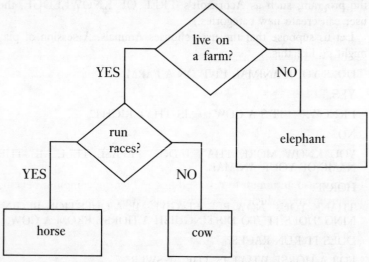

Is it in fact getting cleverer? Obviously not. The algorithm it contains
allows it to elaborate the nodes on its knowledge tree, but it is
entirely dependent on the human to teach it the truth and indeed to
provide it with consistent logic. There is nothing to stop the user from
entering CAT in several places, for instance as an animal which lives
on a farm and again as an animal which does not live on a farm. The
machine will not, given the present form of program, recognize the
inconsistency. There is nothing forcing the human to enter real
animals: fantasies and nonsense are just as readily processed. Experience suggests, however, that users strive towards logic even when
they are dealing in fantasy; unicorns or bats-out-of-hell may be
entered, but they are described and classified as logically as possible.

It is also up to the users to decide how they will interpret the questions they are asked. The question DOES IT LIVE ON A FARM? might mean 'Is it found on a farm?' or 'Is it kept by a farmer?' With the first meaning we would have to include rats and beetles among creatures which live on a farm, but with the second meaning we would only say 'Yes' to creatures like cows, pigs and ducks. Which meaning is correct? The machine will not tell you. I have usually found that groups playing this game in my classes turn to me for a ruling, and may get rather cross with me when I decline to give them one. Eventually they see that they must agree to use one sense of the question, and the reasons for choosing one sense or the other may have less to do with absolute truth and logic than with how other groups playing the game are most likely to understand the meaning. The players are learning to take other language users into account.

In JACKASS the next stage of the game rewards the user for having taught the machine, since the machine uses its classified knowledge to present little 'essays' about each animal. First the user selects an animal from a displayed list by means of a pointer. Now the machine will display something like the following:

THE ELEPHANT

.... LET ME THINK.

AN ELEPHANT IS AN ANIMAL. IT DOESN'T HAVE STRIPES, DOESN'T EAT NUTS, HAS A TRUNK AND DOESN'T LIVE ON A FARM.

There is also an option to reverse roles and let the computer become the quizmaster, which gives a display like this:

THE ANIMAL I AM THINKING OF DOESN'T HAVE STRIPES, DOESN'T EAT NUTS, HAS A TRUNK AND DOESN'T LIVE ON A FARM. WHAT IS IT?

and now the user can point at an animal and get the answer THAT'S RIGHT or I WAS THINKING OF AN ELEPHANT as the case may be. Although the computer is now the question setter, it is using in its questions only information provided by users. If the questions turn out to be difficult, the group can be stimulated into asking why and wondering if a better set of Yes/No questions in the earlier phase of the game might yield a clearer task now.

Morphology

The computer's composition skills are rather limited in this form of the program. It simply goes from the animal node back up the question tree, selecting either DOESN'T plus the verb stem plus the rest of the phrase if it is climbing a negative branch, or verb stem plus -S plus the rest of the phrase if it is climbing an affirmative branch. However, even that process is not as simple as it sounds, since adding a third person -S to an English verb is subject to some interesting morphological constraints. The first challenge one can give to the learners is to find out if the machine knows all the constraints. Can the class catch the computer out, force it to make a mistake? In an early distributed version of the program there was a programming error (a missing RETURN command) which meant that verbs like FLY were turned into FLISES. This was amusing, but quickly led to the question, what would the program do to SAY or PLAY. It got those right. So what kind of error was involved? And what was the rule of English grammar which the program should have used?

The program made use of one other set of morphological rules in order to put AN in front of ELEPHANT and A in front of COW. The rules can be expressed fairly compactly, but not many native speakers of English could state them all without a lot of thought. Consider the cases of UNICORN, UNEXPLORED TERRITORY, HOUR, ONE-TOED SLOTH, and ONAGER. The subroutines which I used to select A or AN and to add -S to verbs derived from what were originally free-standing programs for the 1K ZX81 computer, written by Tim Johns. He used them purely as devices to allow students to explore the morphological rules involved. I deliberately left a few 'holes' in my versions, so that students might try to catch the machine out. In the case of A/AN, for instance, I omitted to 'trap' the case of words or phrases beginning with ONE or ONCE. Although FLISES was just a programming error at first, I have on occasion used the faulty version deliberately in order to get students to think about the possible causes.

Frequency adverbs

Another, more important, omission in the -S ending routine is that I did not try to trap any frequency adverbs. If the user's question is DOES IT EVER EAT BAMBOO?, the machine's statement will be either IT EVERS EAT BAMBOO or IT DOESN'T EVER EAT BAMBOO. It is interesting to note that the negative sentence is acceptable. If the input question had been DOES IT SOMETIMES CATCH MICE?, then both versions of the statement would have been faulty: IT SOMETIMESES CATCH MICE and IT DOESN'T SOMETIMES CATCH MICE. This particular bug could be caught easily enough by providing a list of frequency adverbs which the machine would match against the first word after DOES IT, but having made the match, it is still interesting to consider what the machine should do when it turns the questions into statements. Consider these examples:

DOES IT EVER CATCH MICE?

YES: IT SOMETIMES CATCHES MICE.

NO: IT NEVER CATCHES MICE.

That is clear enough. But what should the negative answer be to the question DOES IT OFTEN CATCH MICE? Is it NEVER or SOMETIMES? Do we have the same problem with ALWAYS? How about the negation of DOES IT SOMETIMES CATCH MICE? Should that be NEVER or ALL THE TIME? And in the following case:

DOES IT USUALLY CATCH MICE?

YES: IT USUALLY CATCHES MICE.

NO: IT DOESN'T USUALLY CATCH MICE.

does the NO answer mean that it tries to catch mice and usually fails, or that it usually catches something else? There is much interesting material for the students to speculate on here. The answers are not to be found in language rules but in real-world truths or in the speaker's mind. I have never, in fact, needed to write this part of the program. Once my students know the program fairly well, all I need to do is to introduce these questions, asking them to imagine they are going to design the next section and take these decisions. They are in effect programming without a computer.

Co-ordination

The next stage of improving the program would be to equip it to break up its little essays into several sentences. We could, for instance, instruct it to put two 'facts' into each sentence, linking them with AND if they are both affirmative or both negative, or with BUT if there is one affirmative and one negative statement. The description of the elephant would now come out as follows:

THE ELEPHANT

AN ELEPHANT IS AN ANIMAL. IT DOESN'T HAVE STRIPES AND DOESN'T EAT NUTS. IT HAS A TRUNK BUT DOESN'T LIVE ON A FARM.

One could equip the program with a reduction rule which will remove repeated verbs in the same sentence, thus turning

IT HAS STRIPES AND HAS CLAWS.

into

IT HAS STRIPES AND CLAWS.

If the machine is given this rule to apply in all cases, however, it will turn

IT DOESN'T HAVE STRIPES AND DOESN'T HAVE CLAWS.

into

IT DOESN'T HAVE STRIPES AND CLAWS.

suggesting that STRIPES and CLAWS are a closely linked pair. Sooner or later, a student should point out that OR is the word to use when a negative has been deleted. (No grammar course, as far as I know, presents this rule in this form.) Another interesting point that should surface in discussion is that the affirmative-negative pattern can be shortened as follows:

IT HAS STRIPES BUT NOT CLAWS.

whereas the negative-affirmative pattern will not work:

IT DOESN'T HAVE STRIPES BUT CLAWS.

This is a possible sentence, but suggests that claws function as a substitute for stripes, and that no animal could have both.

This could lead learners to wonder if there is something a bit odd about the last sentence. In general we allow disconnected notions to be concatenated with AND but we expect a stronger thematic link when two notions are linked by BUT. The sentence

MY SISTER CAN'T PLAY THE PIANO BUT MY BROTHER LIKES CHEESE.

(which I have seen in a language-teaching textbook) rightly arouses mirth. The program, if it performs algorithmically, is bound to generate a large number of such pairs. What can then happen is that learners start to enjoy themselves looking for ludicrous pairings:

IT DOESN'T LIVE IN THE SEA BUT IT EATS RABBITS.
IT LIKES PEOPLE BUT IT DOESN'T FLY.

What are the implications of these? The first suggests that only sea creatures normally eat rabbits, and the second that only flying creatures like people. So now try to think of a sea creature which does eat rabbits, or a flying creature that likes people. If learners start playing with sentences like these, they are forced to think not only about the surface meaning but about the real-world implication. One can do this kind of work without a computer, of course, e.g. by writing simple sentences about ten different animals on the blackboard (making five affirmative statements and five negative ones) and then asking learners to imagine some creature which combines the attributes of two of the animals. One would not need to restrict the subject matter to animals; I have used this technique in intermediate classes with pictures of household objects. Learners enjoy themselves trying to design a radio that irons clothes, for instance.

With some effort it would be possible to anticipate many of the problems thrown up by the JACKASS program and write a version with enough artificial intelligence (e.g. through a semantically tagged lexicon of verbs) to filter out all the nonsense. But what would be the gain? It would mean that learners would never be able to teach the machine falsehoods or nonsense, and would never see falsehoods or nonsense on the screen. At first sight this might seem to be something to applaud. On reflection, however, surely this implies very little respect for the learners' own common sense, and imposes vast restrictions on the learners' imagination. The mere fact that the machine carries out orders in a slave-like and completely unimaginative way can be a liberating factor when a human being comes to use it. There are times when the machine's lack of intelligence shows us things we might never have noticed for ourselves and awakens intelligence and imagination in people who have had little chance to develop them before. This is in contrast to those approaches to language teaching, regrettably common, which assume a teacher who is both proficient in the subject matter and intelligent about deciding how to present it, while also assuming a learner who has no proficiency and no intelligence.

Induction and deduction

If one wants to classify acts of reasoning and learning into deduction and induction, i.e. moving from general to particular or from particular to general, then there is little doubt that programs like JACKASS belong to the inductive approach. JACKASS supplies examples and data, but it is the user who has to create the larger classifications and principles that will make sense of them. Learning can, usually does, involve both deductive and inductive procedures, but styles of teaching usually show a preference for one or the other. I think there can be little doubt that a strongly inductive style of teaching (notice I do not say learning) is rather rare, though one could perhaps find it in the Silent Way, in Total Physical Response, or in a wholehearted application of Krashen's Natural Approach. Such inductive approaches, however, share the characteristic of being carried out in an unaware fashion; the learner is being encouraged to think about the meanings to be conveyed and not about the means of conveying them. The kind of exploratory and problem-solving approach which I have been describing differs by encouraging reflection about the means, an overt analysis of language itself.

This in some ways parallels the difference between the two major deductive approaches: structural or drill-based on the one hand, promoting habit formation while suppressing conscious analysis of language, and cognitive code on the other, allowing attention to be given to the means as well as to the end. We could display this classification as a grid:

	Deductive	Inductive
Unaware	Pattern-practice	Immersion
Aware	Cognitive code	Exploratory

The explicit and aware use of induction is not common in language teaching, except perhaps in the Silent Way. Perhaps we could relate this to the other element missing from much formal tuition but very common in infant learning, conscious linguistic play. Play, however, needs a playmate, a mother, say, or a sibling, or a friend. Teachers are not really fitted for this role; they are too intelligent and take too many initiatives. They bend the rules of the game, often in a well-meaning effort to help.

But that is something the computer will not do. It follows the rules. It is too stupid to do anything else. What we have to realize is that its very stupidity can be turned into an asset, since it releases the learner's intelligence, the learner's hunger for self-knowledge, and the instinct to explore. Perhaps, however, we do not need to use the computer; problem-solving and rule-induction tasks done with pencil and paper may work just as well. We can be grateful to the computer for reminding us what can be done, but it is not essential. What is essential is a pedagogue, a player A who responds but does not interfere or direct the course of argument. Humans play this role reluctantly, but they must learn to do it if exploratory learning is to work. Otherwise they will have to leave it to the computer.

4 The teacher

You can lead a horse to water but you can't make it drink.

(English proverb)

The word *teach* is ambiguous in several ways. In the first place it may be plus or minus intention. There is a difference between 'Mr Jones taught me physics' and 'The audience at the rock concert taught me a lot about human nature.' In the context of institutional teaching we are obviously more likely to use the word in the first sense than the second, but we need to keep the other sense in mind. It is that sense that was meant the Thai student I described on page 3 when he listed the filmstars who had been his 'teachers'. It also describes the role played by the learning environment, which can sometimes be harsh. Like the candle flame which burns the fingers of the inquisitive child, it shows whether an action was 'right' or 'wrong', whether it 'worked' or 'failed', but it does not in general explain why. The explanation has to come from elsewhere and, unless it is offered by an observer, it will usually have to be dug out; to find answers you have to learn to ask questions.

Success

Instruction is the process of giving explanations which have not been asked for, trying to forestall the child's burnt finger by warning of the danger of flames, for instance. But even if we take *teach* to mean *instruct*, we are left with an interesting ambiguity as to whether the word *teach* implies success. In certain contexts an act of teaching is regarded as incomplete until there has been a successful act of learning. If I claim to have taught somebody how to swim, then I must believe that my pupil can now swim; there would be a macabre ungrammaticality about the sentence: 'I taught them how to swim but they all drowned when they jumped into the swimming pool.' We remove the ungrammaticality if we replace 'taught them' by 'gave them some lessons on'. In this context the terms are clearly not identical in meaning.

The implication that teaching has been successful is strongly made when we are talking about single skills or knacks, such as swimming or riding a bicycle. It is less strong but still present when we are talking about procedures, as in 'I taught them how to change a wheel.' It becomes distinctly fuzzy when we talk about precepts or ethics. How much success is implied if we say 'I taught them the difference between right and wrong' or 'I taught them never to start the lathe unless the safety shield was in place'?

When we reach the level of teaching facts rather than skills, teaching *that* rather than teaching *how*, then we can always mitigate our implied claim to have succeeded by invoking the learner's memory or comprehension failures. 'I taught him that computer books are classified as information science, but he still keeps putting them with engineering.' But it is when we come to curricular subjects that the implication of success vanishes almost completely. 'I taught him German for five years, but he never learned a thing.' That sentence may be sad, but it is not ungrammatical. In the context of school subjects, *teach* and *give lessons on* are fully equivalent.

Responsibility

If you have an industrial view of teaching, that so much labour ought to result in so many products, then this state of affairs is going to seem shocking. The industrial view is related to the empty-vessel model; it assumes that the teacher is the only active participant in the process and that the teacher's time and effort is what determines the quantity of learning. However, even the most quantitively-minded critic must allow that the learner can block out teaching by not listening or not remembering. Unsuccessful learners can then be thought of as like patients who pour away the medicine because it tastes nasty; the doctor does not get the blame if they do not get well.

Yet it seems to me that the teacher, and especially the teacher in a compulsory education system, is responsible not just for seeing that subject matter gets taught but for seeing that learners actually learn. If something is going wrong, it is up to the teacher to find out why; if the learners are, like the patients, pouring away the medicine, then the teacher should try a different medicine or use a different method to persuade the learners to take it. It is usually the teacher who, thanks to training and maturity, is more able to change direction and try new approaches. One mark of the difference between good and bad teachers is their attitude to mistakes. The bad teacher gets angry; the mistake is seen as an insult: 'I've told you that five hundred times!'. The good teacher, by contrast, treats a mistake as something inherently interesting, a phenomenon to be explained and an indicator of a different way of getting the point across.

Roles

The metaphor on which this book is based suggests only two models of teaching behaviour, magister and pedagogue, with the crucial difference between them being the amount of control exercised. The magister fixes the order of events and attempts to exercise control through issuing instructions and securing responses, which he then evaluates. The pedagogue responds and serves, but neither initiates nor evaluates. But magister and pedagogue are labels for attitudes and approaches to tasks, not the tasks themselves. We can enumerate several roles or tasks which human teachers undertake, each of which may have elements of the magister or the pedagogue in them. For instance, the teacher can function as lecturer, manager, referee, play-mate, facilitator, model, informant, or diagnostician. In some cases the role demands a magister or a pedagogue; in others the blend is a matter of personal style.

Magister roles

The three roles which are most heavily magisterial are those of manager, diagnostician, and facilitator, since these are the ones which demand intervention and judgement. In the modern classroom most teachers of language would see their major role as that of manager. What we do in classrooms may range from highly-controlled activities, such as drills and comprehension questions, to 'free' activities such as role play and discussion. All these activities, however, have a struc-ture or routine, a beginning, middle and end, and there must, there-fore, be somebody in charge who knows what the structure is. The teacher can, of course, delegate the management task to a student, getting the student to come to the front of the class and pose the questions or lead the discussion, but the act of delegation is a management decision and one which can be reversed when necessary. Management also implies management of resources. If a particular book or visual aid is going to be needed, it is the teacher's responsi-bility to see that it is there.

The teacher functioning as diagnostician is preparing for the management task, gathering evidence for the management decisions he or she will have to make. This occurs formally in class tests, but should also occur informally during many kinds of class activity, as the teacher tries constantly to read the signals the class sends out. This is one area in which a human teacher is still immeasurably superior to a machine; we have many more channels of communication open, and a vast amount of cultural awareness and common sense which lets us make sense of what students tell us. Teachers who do not listen to their pupils are throwing away their greatest advantage over machines, and should indeed be worried about whether the computer can replace them.

The role of facilitator or motivator is to ensure that the members of the class get things to do which are relevant and enjoyable, whether as individuals or as a group. The teacher also has to convey, either overtly or covertly, why the subject is worth studying at all. It is up to the teacher to project the image of an enthusiast who wants the learners to 'join the club' of people who command the same skills. This is often simply a matter of securing respect and affection. Several seasons of interviewing applicants for college places have shown me how often students pick a subject because of their personal admiration of an individual teacher. The reverse, of course, is equally true; our dislike of an individual can lead us to dismiss the subject matter they have tried to teach us.

Pedagogue roles

The most important pedagogue role is that of linguistic model, since the teacher's language may be the only exposure the class has to spontaneous and meaningful use of the language. It is then up to the teacher to show that the language 'works'. The teacher acts as demonstrator in very much the same way as the sports coach, showing how things are done and how the right way works better than the wrong way. Although this is a pedagogue role, it is one that for the time being can only be done by a human being, since the machines are not yet clever enough to use language meaningfully except in limited domains.

The role of lecturer, apparently the most magisterial, has paradoxically some pedagogue characteristics. It is while lecturing that you have least control over whether anyone is actually learning from what you say. Lecturing is often carried out not so much because it is the best way of presenting information as to satisfy the lecturer that the ground has been covered; the teacher can then complain 'But I told you that last week' when a student shows ignorance. A related role is that of consultant or informant, supplying information on demand or directing the learner to the place where it can be found. It is the mark of a good informant not to give more information than is asked for, not to turn an answer into a lecture. It is also a mark of confidence and expertise to be ready to admit what one does not know. The good teacher is often the one who can say, 'I don't know. Let's look it up.'

The only roles in which the machine is palpably superior to the human teacher are those of playmate and referee, and the reason for this superiority is that those roles demand rule-bound behaviour. In those areas of language where we are dealing with language rules and want to use inductive game-like teaching strategies, i.e. when we want learners to induce the rules by observing their effects, then we need a teacher who will not bend the rules in order to be kind. This is a role which the machine plays very well.

Teacher training

The multiplicity of roles complicates the professional training of a language teacher. It is obvious that one cannot handle training just by equipping teachers with a repertoire of techniques; they need not only techniques but also the means of deciding when one technique is appropriate. The techniques can be learned either from instruction or from observation. The decision-making skills, on the other hand, probably cannot be taught magisterially, but have to come from analysing what happens in classes. This is generally provided by periods of observation and teaching practice, but there is one other way in which potential teachers can gain experience, and that is as learners. Since their own experience as language learners may by the time of their training be a distant memory, it may be necessary for them to learn something new. It is for this reason that a number of British university courses now include as part of the training of an EFL teacher a requirement that the trainee learns a new foreign language and keeps a diary of the experience.

Cryptomethodology

In the case when the trainee is not a native speaker, then the period of training is likely to include advanced work in the language itself. This provides the opportunity for what I call cryptomethodology. I gave it this name because, in a number of places where I taught, the official syllabus provided a ludicrously small number of hours devoted to methods training as such. It was, I felt, necessary to smuggle some additional methodology into the course, which I did as follows. Each lesson in language would end ten minutes early and would be followed by a period of analysis and discussion of the lesson itself. I would write a few questions on the board to get the discussion started, but would then leave for five minutes; if my own performance was to be analysed, it was not right for me to stay around.

Sauce for the gander

The result of this work, as far as I could tell, was not only a better grasp of the objectives and workings of some pieces of teaching technique, but also an improved grasp of certain areas of language itself. The invitation to reflect on and discuss a language-learning experience seemed to have value in letting the new piece of learning settle. One reason that I adopted this approach was to avoid being accused of providing sauce for the goose but not sauce for the gander. In many teacher-training environments the trainers seem quite ready to teach methodology while themselves using quite the opposite methodology, to give lectures deploring the use of lectures, to talk about the importance of exposure to authentic language but to use abstract talk instead of practical demonstration themselves. I mentioned at the beginning of this chapter one ambiguity of the word 'teach', that it can be plus or minus intention. Teacher trainers must be effective teachers in both senses, in what they say and in what they do.

Respect

A magisterial approach to teacher training often seems to go hand in hand with a lack of respect for the ability or intelligence of the trainees. It is unfortunately the case that in many countries teaching is underpaid and attracts students with lower academic grades than other professions. Teachers for the most part are employed by governments, and they have to be employed in large numbers, which means that there is always a strong economic case against paying them properly. It is also unfortunate that language teachers are all too often let loose on their careers with inadequate grasp of the language they are going to teach. One would think that the answer to this would be to give them first-rate language courses, so that they can project an image of success. What actually happens is the opposite; they get more of the standard language courses which have already served them so badly, and are trained in a rigid syllabus and methodology, since the authorities cannot trust them to make independent decisions. The ultimate insult comes when they are given a prescribed textbook which is 'teacher-proof', i.e. one in which the teacher's book has detailed lesson plans amounting to lesson scripts, ensuring that each class period is filled with routines. 'Teacher-proof' has ominous echoes of 'idiot-proof', and when you treat professional people as idiots, they begin to see themselves that way.

Teacher training and language laboratories

These are mistakes we should be trying to avoid when it comes to teacher training in a machine age, but we also need to beware of an earlier error, namely avoiding the mistakes by avoiding the training. In the heyday of the language laboratory very little pre-service training was ever given in either the theory or the practice of language laboratory use. Instead most training was in the form of short in-service courses, given to teachers who had volunteered. Even training colleges which owned laboratories hardly ever trained their students to handle the teacher's console. No doubt the reasoning was that only a few students were likely to have access to laboratories in the schools they were assigned to and that, even if they did, the school would probably already have appointed a staff member to be in charge.

One result of this was that those schools which owned a laboratory were often dependent on a single enthusiastic staff member to keep it going. If that person left, there might be nobody trained to take over. Some of the worst consequences were seen in institutions in developing countries whenever the enthusiast was an expatriate on a two-year contract. However expert these expatriates were in running the laboratory itself, very few of them were capable of setting up systems which could survive after their own departure.

Who takes charge?

We seem to be in some danger of making the same mistake with computers. Most training courses in CALL are in-service courses rather than initial training; it is currently thought more important to give short courses to practising teachers who are already supplied with machines rather than train new teachers who may not have access to computers for some time. The result, as with the laboratory, is that it is isolated enthusiasts who are handling whatever CALL effort is made in schools, and that they often have difficulty in handing over or sharing the work with other teachers who have the relevant background.

Whether you find this satisfactory or worrying will depend on the importance you attach to computer work in language learning. You may well feel that the enthusiasts can safely be left to carry out their experimental work while the bulk of the profession gets on with face-to-face interactions with learners. But there are two dangers. One, less important, is that useful innovations will be resisted because teachers feel they have not been consulted and are not equipped to evaluate the innovation. The other, far more serious, is that spurious innovations, supported by large government and commercial investment, will be foisted on a teaching profession that is not trained to resist them.

Teacher training for CALL

However some teacher-training establishments are beginning to include computer work in pre-service training courses. The way they set about providing the training varies, but it usually includes some combination of lectures, practice in operating the machines, practice with word-processing, the creation of exercises with an authoring system, and BASIC programming. The duration varies from half a day to the equivalent of several weeks. The subject has not yet reached the level of specialization where it can be made the central component of a year-long course, although graduate students are allowed or may even be encouraged to write dissertations in the area of CALL. Perhaps the most important product of pre-service training will be not great skill in handling the machines but simply demystification of computers, removing the element of fear. The skill will come with practice, but people who have never had a chance to experiment with computers in a protected environment are often afraid to take the first step later.

Should teachers learn to program?

Computer training is often equated with BASIC programming. This comes in for a good deal of criticism, particularly from computer specialists who regard BASIC as an inefficient and unsuitable language. They would prefer either a more limited language dedicated to education, such as PILOT, or a more structured language such as PASCAL. Some experts recommend the Artificial Intelligence languages LISP and PROLOG, as these will make it easier to develop software which breaks away from drill and quiz formats.

This whole argument, however, begs the question of whether it is worth learning to program at all. Teachers are not all trained to write textbooks, although they are expected to be able to prepare tests, occasional supplementary exercises, and comprehension questions on reading texts. By analogy, training English teachers to program may look like a cheap way of securing ELT software to supplement published sources, but the results are likely to be disappointing. Very few teachers will learn enough or become interested enough after a short course in programming to produce software worth using in their own classes, let alone distributing to other teachers. There may be a handful who turn out to have a special talent and become expert software writers. This would certainly be welcome, since software should be written by people with subject expertise as well as computer expertise. However, giving short courses to all teachers may not be the most efficient way of finding the next generation of programmers.

A different reason why teachers should learn to program is that it allows them to grapple with a problem-solving approach to language. Before one can make a computer display language or process language, even at the level of matching an input with a stored word, one has to work out from the computer's point of view what a word is and what it means to say that two words are the same. In a sense one has to teach the computer, and in the process one is likely to learn. If nothing else, one may learn some tolerance of learners' errors and some respect for learners' intelligence.

The teacher as learner

This, then, is the case I would make for making CALL training widespread: not to prepare teachers to adopt CALL universally, but to teach them something about the language which they would not be likely to learn in other ways. In the process I would expect them to go through some frustration and some feelings of triumph when a problem is solved. If they have enjoyed the task, I would hope that they can see that the students they will eventually teach are entitled to experience the same enjoyment if the opportunity can be provided. Providing the opportunity may not necessarily require the use of machines.

You can lead a horse to water, the proverb reminds us, but you cannot make it drink. Perhaps, if we taste the water ourselves, we will become better at leading our horses to water they will find palatable.

5 The book

This too will be your fate. Your doddering old age will be spent in teaching the elements of Latin to boys in remote corners of the world.

Horace, commenting on what would happen to his own verse, Epistles I.xx. 17–18, quoted in Kelly (1969)

In earlier chapters I have raised the question of whether computers can perform the functions of a teacher. I want now to ask whether computer software can provide language learners with what they would otherwise get from books. Of course it is necessary to find out first what the book does. In the context of language learning, 'the book' usually means either a textbook, also known as a coursebook, or a collection of texts known, confusingly, as the 'reader'. To avoid ambiguity I shall refer to the latter as the reading book.

The textbook

The textbook's role is magisterial. It imposes an order and is normally designed to be worked through in sequence. It is often used as a syllabus: what is in the textbook gets taught, and what is not there is neither taught nor tested. It may contain statements about the language which are to be memorized and believed, certainly not disputed. (Some students get upset when asked to correct misprints or errors in their textbooks; writing in a printed book is felt to be desecration.) The textbook probably contains exercises which the learners must carry out in a certain way, and a list of answers which are deemed right, all other answers by implication being wrong. Like the good human magister, it is relied on for comfort and certainty. Students are likely to complain if a teacher decides to teach units from the textbook in an order different from the printed one or to omit substantial sections.

The main coursebook that students use often seems to become synonymous with the language itself. 'What are you studying?' 'Kernel One.' This is quite a burden of responsibility for a book to carry, since even a very large book or a series of books is meagre in comparison with the whole of the subject. A dictionary can list and define all the words which a learner will ever need or be likely to encounter. A grammar book can state in a highly abstract form and then exemplify virtually all the permissible patternings of a language. A coursebook, however, must try to achieve rather more than either of these. It has to take each formal component of a language and put it into situations which make the meaning clear. It has to show how far patterns can be generalized. It also has to provide materials for practice to replace the experience of language which infants get from hundreds of thousands of attempts to communicate and from thousands of hours of exposure to language and language play.

The reading book

A reading book, unlike a coursebook, neither fixes an order nor determines a syllabus. It may be a single work, a novel for example, in which case one would normally begin at the beginning and read to the end, but there would be no language progression within the book making this necessary. If it is an anthology of separate pieces, then there is no obligation on anyone to adopt a particular order. It may have some magisterial trappings added to it, such as questions and exercises after each chapter, but it is more likely that it only has a glossary. In most cases the author will claim that the reading book is enjoyable to read; it is there to provide experience of language, but the experience should be motivating. All of these features cast it in something more like the pedagogue role.

A reading book is also seen as having a much more limited function than the textbook. Teachers will usually regard it as something to help in the development of reading skills alone, whereas they see the textbook as an aid to the development of all language skills. (They may be quite wrong, of course. Their learners may be using the reading book as comprehensible input and thereby increasing their active command of grammar and vocabulary, while at the same time the textbook is having little effect on their productive skills. This is certainly what the Input Hypothesis would predict.)

Intensive and extensive reading

At early stages of learning, reading is the mechanical process of attaching sound to written symbols. At some point learners should reach the stage where they can attach meaning directly to the symbols without having to puzzle out the sounds first. From this point onwards most teaching manuals and methodology courses draw a distinction between intensive reading and extensive reading. Passages within a textbook would usually be intended for intensive reading, while the reading book supplies material for extensive reading. I would prefer to use a different pair of terms and to talk about 'study' and 'reading'.

Study

The reason why I prefer the term 'study' to 'intensive reading' is that I doubt whether intensive reading as practised in foreign-language classrooms deserves to be called reading at all. Proficient readers normally approach a book or a document with one of two distinct attitudes: the text is either something to be read or something to be studied. Studying entails that we look at the same piece of text several times, and return to it on different occasions. The speed at which we process the text may be rather slow, perhaps only 60 or 70 words a minute overall. We tend to store the information we obtain, either in our minds or in notes, using the same form of words as was used in the original work. A book we have studied is often a book we can quote.

Reading

Real-life reading differs from study in three important ways. In the first place, information obtained by reading is hardly ever retained verbatim; if asked to talk about something we have read, what we produce will be a paraphrase. Secondly, reading must be carried out at speed. The minimum speed is usually a little faster than a normal speaking speed, say 180 words per minute; slower than this and reading turns into study or is abandoned because it brings no pleasure. Finally, reading demands fresh material: if I hand you yesterday's newspaper or last month's magazine, you are likely to say 'No thanks, I've read it.' All these characteristics (retention by paraphrase, fast speed, and fresh material) tend to be absent from classroom reading.

Destroying reading

Reading, i.e. extensive reading, is usually included as a target skill in any syllabus, while study skills only appear explicitly among the objectives of specialized courses. Yet, paradoxically, although we want our students to learn to read, we only train them to study. The reading book may be offered as a way out of this dilemma; it provides material for extensive reading which can be done out of class. What teachers often fail to realize is how easily they can destroy reading. All they have to do is to assign texts to be read and announce that there will be a test including questions of detail; this automatically converts reading into study. It may seem that if the assigned texts are long enough, they will have to be read because there will not be enough time to study them. In the event students will solve the problem in a different way: they will simply study as much as they have time for. If you want evidence for this, look at the shelves of any British Council library overseas, in particular the classic fiction. You will find that most volumes have the first fifteen or so pages heavily annotated with underlinings and translations written in the margins. From page twenty-five onwards the margins will be as white as snow.

Computers and reading

Since the computer's natural role is that of pedagogue, and since the reading book is, or should be, in a pedagogue relationship to the learner, it might seem to follow that the computer can be used as a delivery system for reading matter and will thus help develop a reading skill. In practice this turns out to be a fallacy for two reasons. Firstly there is no need to use a computer screen to do a job which is already done very well and much more cheaply with paper and ink. Secondly it is gradually becoming clear that reading from a screen is a rather different activity from reading from the printed page.

To know why this is so, it is worth remembering just how great an investment we have made in accustoming ourselves to the conventions of printing and book design. Books are pleasant objects to hold. People may forget the publisher, the author, or even the title of a book they have enjoyed, but will remember its shape and the colour of the binding. We enjoy the flexibility of being able to hold a book in our hands or lay it on a table or desk. To find the most comfortable focusing distance for our eyes, we move the book with our hands, whereas with a computer screen we need to move our whole body. In this respect reading a screen is akin to reading notices pinned on a board.

Typography

It is not until we are faced with something different that we realize how much we rely on conventions of typography. We are used to seeing black letters on a white background, whereas computer screens more often give us light letters on a dark background. We think of a page as a vertical shape, rather than the horizontal one which is the norm for computer screens. In printed books we expect to see both margins justified, and, although we may not be conscious of it, we feel more comfortable if the print is proportionally spaced, for instance, with the wide letters such as *m* and *w* given more space than the narrow ones, such as *i* and *j*. Very few computer screens display true proportional spacing, and justifying the right-hand margin can, therefore, only be achieved by putting long gaps between some of the words, which is known to reduce legibility. Perhaps the most important difference between the two media is in the quantity of text within one's vision. Most computer screens display only a hundred or so words comfortably; any more and the screen becomes too crowded or the letters too small. Yet there is a certain size of page that feels right for a particular type of material: if we are reading a novel, we expect to see about 450 words on a page or 900 on a double spread, and may feel upset if we get very much more or less than this. What is more, we expect to see the full contents of the page all the time; we do not want it revealed to us a line at a time, or scrolled up through a notional window.

Finding the place

We also like the convenience of being able to mark the place we have reached when we put a book aside, either by putting in a slip of paper or by placing it face down and open on the table. Most important of all, though, is the ability to flick back and forward, to scan the book for its chapter headings, or to refer back to a paragraph. Significantly we often remember the paragraph we are looking for by its position on the page rather than by its relation to other content. The bound pages of the modern book make this very easy. We would not choose to revert to the papyrus scroll libraries of classical times, and yet this is roughly what using a computer screen for long texts makes us do.

Flexibility

The one disadvantage that books have is that they are rigid; once consigned to print, they become fixed. Computer text, by contrast, is very easy to change. Since it is stored on re-usable magnetic media, there are no economies of scale to worry about. A publisher does not need to print a vast number of copies, and, if a faulty version is sold, one simply asks the purchaser to send back the disk and then copies the corrected version on top of the faulty one. The software may even include a provision for the user to make editorial changes without defacing the product, though this is rare.

The computer as reading aid

If reading and study are distinct activities, and if nearly all explicit training turns out to be training to study, how can reading be taught? In practice the best thing a teacher can do is to ensure that reading brings rewards, which may take the form of enjoyment, of enhanced knowledge, or of success in competitive activities which necessitate reading. Teaching reading may largely be a matter of convincing learners that they will enjoy it if they do more of it. If the computer is to play any part in this, it must be with materials which are enthralling to read or in which the reading is a condition of enjoying some other experience, such as solving a problem or winning a game, which is itself highly motivating. The most interesting developments are in the field of dynamic story-telling, exemplified by programs like ZORK, and in text adventures. The actual reading need not be done from a screen; the great success of the Melbourne House program, THE HOBBIT, has had the incidental effect of sending many new readers to Tolkien's book. The foreign-language learner has so far not had much benefit from this, since hardly any programs have been written with language simple enough to be read with comfort by an intermediate-level learner, and language which is too difficult is never read – it is studied.

Top-down and bottom-up

The distinction between reading and study brings to mind another distinction, familiar in programming jargon, between two approaches to problem solving. The top-down approach starts with the most general description of the task and elaborates it progressively, while the bottom-up approach takes the smallest identifiable components of the task and combines them into solutions to parts of the problem and ultimately to the whole problem if possible. Neither approach is necessarily right, though you should be aware which one you are using. A top-down approach to the teaching of reading would be to require learners to read in quantity and variety and hope that the necessary skills will develop with experience. It says implicitly, 'When you have understood the writer's message, you will be able to notice, select and use the details.' A bottom-up approach would provide separate exercises to train learners in all identifiable sub-skills and hope that the overall skill will be present when all the sub-skills have been mastered. This approach says implicitly, 'When you have grasped the details, you will be able to understand the writer's message.' Notice that each approach contains an element of hope.

Reading programs

Software which claims to teach reading sometimes seems to be neither top-down nor bottom-up, but somewhere in between. It often takes the form of texts broken up into short pages of seventy words or so, plus banks of exercises. The exercises can include focusing questions to be tackled before reading, vocabulary work either in the form of a quiz or else simply a look-up table, and then comprehension questions or questions about the meaning in context of particular words and phrases, all to be answered when the reading is finished. You often find graphics used either in explanatory diagrams or, more commonly, purely as a motivator. The reading activity itself may incorporate branching, so that learners are presented with different outcomes to a story depending on the choices they make. There may also be an element of speed training, with the text being displayed for a measured time, or else with the reader allowed as much time as he or she wants but having the time taken reported afterwards. The weakest part of the package is usually the comprehension questions, just as it is in many textbooks. The questions can very often be answered without sight of the text they are supposed to be testing, and so there is very little incentive to read. The complete activity is highly fragmented and tends to draw in a variety of skills and strategies in a random fashion. It is very likely that the learner will feel that the texts are objects to be studied rather than sources of information or entertainment.

Reading pacers

In spite of all the drawbacks of computer text, computers can be turned into simple reading pacers to measure and perhaps improve reading speed. Reading speed is an interesting and still rather controversial topic. The speed at which one reads has nothing to do with the rate at which one's eyes move. Indeed, one cannot read at all when the eye is moving, but only when it stops to take in a word or phrase. Each stop is called a fixation, and research shows that all readers make more or less the same number of fixations, namely about four per second. Reading speed depends on two things: how many words one takes in at each fixation, and how many regressions, or fixations on words already read, one makes. The good reader takes in long phrases and regresses only occasionally. The bad reader takes in one word at a time and makes frequent regressions. Of course, there may be many other reasons for reading badly, such as trying to read material which is too difficult, but the habit of word-by-word reading is certainly one factor.

To experience the way a bad reader reads, imagine that the following sentence is being revealed to you one word at a time:

WHAT

WHAT DID

WHAT DID SHE

WHAT DID SHE HIT

WHAT DID SHE HIT HIM

WHAT DID SHE HIT HIM FOR?

Clearly you are having to do six times as much work to understand this sentence as you would if you had been given the whole sentence at once. Moreover, although the first four words apparently form a complete phrase which means something, the addition of the fifth word turns it into an ungrammatical and meaningless fragment, and you are almost bound to check back to see if you have understood the beginning of the sentence properly. This is one reason for the bad reader's frequent regressions.

HOPALONG

It is a fairly straightforward task to write a program which displays text on the screen broken up into phrases, though it is up to the person typing in the text to choose the phrase boundaries. In a program my wife and I have developed in Bristol, called HOPA-LONG, the text is printed in a recessive colour (blue on black) and each phrase in turn is highlighted in yellow, the eye being drawn through the text by the highlight. The pace can be changed at any point by touching one of two keys, and all the students are asked to do is to find the speed at which they are most comfortable. They can halt the process to check their speed at any point, or go back to the beginning if they feel they are losing the thread. We are using texts of around 1,000 words, occupying nine or ten successive screens, and have included as much variety of style and subject matter in the libraries of texts as we can. Research is currently in progress to find out what effect the difficulty level and subject matter will have on each reader's choices.

Mechanical reading pacers known as tachistoscopes have been used in the training of reading skills for many years, but they now seem to have fallen into disrepute. These devices ran a fixed size window down a text which was otherwise obscured, thus preventing regression altogether. The computer pacer, HOPALONG, has two advantages: first, it presents the text in meaningful chunks rather than what will fit into an arbitrary size of window; and, second, although it discourages regression, it does not prevent it. It remains to be seen whether it will have any effect on the reading skills of the overseas students who are participating in the experiment.

The computer as study aid

The disadvantages of the computer as a medium for reading and the training of reading apply much less strongly to study and activities based on text study. When we study text, we do not need to look at large segments at a time, so the shape and size of the screen are no drawback. The unattractiveness of computer text is offset by the way pieces of the text can be highlighted and the text as a whole manipulated. To ask the machine to manipulate text is a true use of the computer as slave, in this case as copyist or scribe. It relieves human teachers of one part of their work which is usually complete drudgery: the task of preparing materials. Consider what happens when you put together a cloze exercise. If you are lucky enough to have access to the right machines, you take a photocopy of a text, white out the words you want the students to guess, and then photocopy the resulting document. If you are less lucky, you prepare the text on a typewriter, in which case you must correct any errors you make and always face the risk of not noticing some of the copying errors you have made. To create a sentence reordering exercise you would have to take a copy of the text, cut it up with scissors and paste each sentence onto a piece of card. The end product of your labour is one exercise for one class.

The computer as scribe

The computer can make light of all this labour provided it can be carried out by rule and requires no decisions which are dependent on meaning. If the words to be deleted are at fixed intervals or random intervals, or are chosen by length, or are matched up to some pre-existing list, such as a list of all the English prepositions, the machine will carry out the manipulation in a few seconds at most. It can even make some context checks and perhaps distinguish *before* used as a preposition from *before* used as an adverb, for instance. In the case of the reordering exercise the machine will be quite capable of identifying sentence boundaries provided they are reliably indicated by punctuation or spacing, but will not be able to use common sense to deal with unforeseen cases. It would be likely to treat 'Col. John Smith' as two sentences, since it contains a full stop followed by a space and a capital letter. A human editor will be needed to check the computer's decisions, but that work is easy once the computer has undertaken the major drudgery of putting together the exercise.

What we can expect from the computer, then, is a great increase in the variety of available exercise materials, particularly those based on playing with texts. There is a vast number of possible variations in the basic technique of mutilating a text and asking a learner to restore the original. We can delete part of the text, or indeed the whole text (as in STORYBOARD, discussed in Chapter 1). We can insert spurious letters, words or whole sentences which have to be detected and removed. We can replace letters or words. We can reorder letters, words or sentences. The point of all this activity is not to train students to read but to have them look at text as a puzzle to be solved and, in the process, learn something about how text is put together.

Using a word-processor for exercises

We can even do many of these things without having to use special software. One activity which I have several times carried out with a standard word-processor is to type in a passage of first-person narrative. I then use the search-and-replace command to change all occurrences of 'I', 'me', 'my' and 'mine' into '***'. My students' task is to edit the text in order to turn it into third-person narrative about a character called, say, John Smith. It is not just a matter of putting 'he', 'him' or 'his' in each slot. Learners will also have to decide whether to change any of the starred gaps into a name rather than a pronoun, since, if the words 'he' and 'his' are used in the text to refer to other characters, a pronoun may be ambiguous. Unforeseen problems can arise. In one text which I used recently with a group of teachers we encountered an interpolated 'I believe' in what was otherwise past tense narrative. To change that mechanically into 'he believes' would have led to something stylistically very odd, so most members of the group paraphrased the sentence to begin 'He felt that . . .' or 'He was sure that . . .'. Even with a group of intermediate learners one could expect somebody to notice and comment on problems of this kind.

Reordering

All word-processors include a block-move command which is the easiest way to reorder sentences or paragraphs. The resulting text can be printed out for students to work on away from the machine, or students can work at the machine, using the same command to put the text back in the right order. The purpose of this kind of work is not so much a direct improvement in editing skills, though that may well be a valuable spin-off. It is rather to get learners to think about what makes a piece of text work.

Private experience

Until now text-based exercises have been relatively hard to find in bulk. One effect of this has been that all the learners tend to do the same set of tasks, often working on them together in class. The large class may be a good arena for many forms of language activity, but it tends not to be suitable for work which entails problem solving, speculation, or trial and error. If questions are put publicly, there is a reluctance to give an answer you are not sure of in case you make a fool of yourself. What the computer can do is provide so much material and so many ways of tackling it that learners can work on their own and in small groups, sharing the discoveries they make with others who have not done the same work.

A very similar advantage has been claimed for the language laboratory in the teaching of literature. Headphones and glass-fronted booths seal off the learner in a private cell, which makes the practice of communication quite unrealistic. However, the laboratory provides a very private place in which to think and try to answer questions of opinion, and this may make it a good place in which to encounter a literary work. Following up an idea originally proposed by Anthony Howatt and John Webb, at least two institutions that I know of (the Oslo Extra-Mural Board and Prasanmitr Teacher Training College in Bangkok) experimented with tapes of readings of short works, such as poems or scenes from plays, together with background information. At several points in the tape listeners were asked to write down their own opinions. Students worked through these tapes in the language laboratory, and this was followed up by a class discussion, which often seemed more animated than in more conventional literature classes.

Magister or pedagogue?

Even in types of exercise where there is a right answer, such as text rebuilding or reordering, the computer is not acting as magister. It is playing a game by a set of rules, but that in itself does not amount to making a judgement or taking control. The programs, too, lend themselves to a great variety of uses, but these uses have to be devised and initiated by a human, either teacher or learner. Most text programs come as 'authoring systems' with only a few example texts supplied. Somebody has to type in new texts, and that may be the teacher or, perhaps, one group of learners setting a challenge to another. In the latter case the group entering the texts know they have to be accurate, since the people who eventually use their texts will complain if there are errors. They also have to think about the kinds of text which will surprise or interest or puzzle the next group, all of which is a relevant kind of thinking for language learners to be doing. The point of any text-reconstruction exercise is not to train students to read but to train them to be curious about how text is put together. What they in fact learn depends on which texts are selected (and selection remains firmly a human function carried out by teachers or learners) and on what they actually notice and remember. That there is a good chance that texts will be learned is attested by experiences like these, reported by a teacher using TRAY, a text reconstruction exercise of the STORYBOARD type:

> ... the end-of-lesson bell interrupted our deliberations, and we had to return to the text two days later. Knowing the limited memory span of my charges, we started from scratch again: it was stunning to find that many of the pupils could recite the parts of the passage we had uncovered two days before almost word-for-word, and they had been considering some of the more difficult gaps since the previous lesson.
>
> (Moore 1986, p. 54)

Remember that verbatim recall is a characteristic of study rather than reading.

Teachers use programs like STORYBOARD in many different ways. A class can be given a chapter to read and a summary of the chapter to tackle as a STORYBOARD exercise. This certainly gives an extra reason for reading the main text carefully. STORYBOARD has been used by teachers of translation, with the first-language text on paper and a target-language version on screen. Similarly learners can be given diagrams, graphs or tables and a STORYBOARD passage which is a prose comment on the graphic material. The program has been used by young learners with learning difficulties and by intelligent and well-motivated graduates. Very few of these applications were foreseen when I devised the program. None of them could have taken place if the program had been in full magisterial control.

Computers and books

The arrival of computers is bound to affect the way we use books, but I do not expect them to make books obsolete. On the contrary, I foresee no decrease in the demand for books for reading, since the computer screen serves that function rather poorly, and a likely increase in the demand for paper dictionaries, reference grammars and encyclopedias, since the machine stimulates curiosity and drives learners to all kinds of external sources of information in the search for solutions to problems or challenges which will beat the machine. The one kind of book which may eventually be replaced by the computer is the workbook, but only because the machine supplies in bulk and variety what the workbook provides in meagre quantities.

Meanwhile various attempts to turn books into computer software have perhaps been valuable in reminding us what books are and what we use them for. Books resemble computers in being essentially passive; we can put them back on the shelf as readily as we can switch off the power. But books, unlike computers, are linear; the order in which their content is displayed has been fixed before they reach us. We can, of course, choose to tackle the content in a different order, but books are normally written on the assumption that they will be read from front to back and will not give us any feedback about the order we are using, will not warn us if we miss vital information by omitting a chapter, for instance. Computers, in contrast, are responsive, waiting for the user's decision before selecting the next message to display. This can be liberating, giving us more choices about what to do next, but it can also limit freedom. We cannot browse through programs quite as freely as we can browse through books. One can always 'cheat' with a detective story by reading the last chapter first, but one cannot usually do the same with a computer adventure.

The very linearity of a book can be turned to advantage. Textbooks control the order of presentation of facts and help a teacher maintain structure in a course. Reading books are channels of communication, and are read because we enjoy them or need to understand the messages in them; part of the author's message may well be the order in which the content is presented. A lot of learning demands authority such as is provided by the magister or the textbook, or needs communication to engross the learner, such as is given by the well-written reading book. It is only when we need responsiveness rather than authority or communication that we have to call on the machine. Meanwhile the printed book remains a highly appropriate technology for most learning purposes.

6 The test

It is often said of institutional tests that they are 'fair' or 'unfair'. It is worth considering what these terms imply.

If I weigh myself or take my temperature, I may complain if I think the results are inaccurate. I may find the results unexpected or unwelcome. However, I would probably not call them unfair. The same would be true if a doctor measured my blood pressure or used an electrocardiograph to investigate my heart. The one occasion on which I might be tempted to call the doctor or his instruments unfair would be if I was being tested for blood alcohol content after a road accident and knew that the results might be used by the police to prosecute me. Obviously I would want to take advantage of any legal margin of doubt which might save me from punishment; if the test result was in my favour, I would not be likely to question it.

When teachers or institutions administer tests, the tests are usually thought of as more like the blood alcohol test than, say, taking one's temperature. It is the institution, not the learners, who will use the test results in their decision making. The tests are not primarily for the learners' benefit or information, although there may be benefit to the learner in passing a test. Students are not consulted about the test, not asked what kinds of questions they would like to answer. Results are not known immediately, and may never be fully explained. All of this makes such tests highly magisterial. Control lies away from the learner.

Instruments of power

Tests may also provide the teacher with a way of asserting dominance, feeding the hunger for power which exists to some extent in nearly all of us. In its extreme form this emerges as the wish to humiliate learners by exposing their inadequacy. I have heard recent accounts of senior university professors who fail their complete class, trying to convey the message, 'How can you miserable upstarts possibly satisfy me, the great scholar?' They neglect the implications of their action: that they have failed to give to the class any of the skills and insights which they are expected to, that they have failed to earn their salary. Students, however, sometimes fight back against this autocracy by demanding that teachers stick narrowly to the part of the syllabus which is to be tested. One of the most depressing questions a teacher can hear is 'Will this be in the test?' – with the clear implication that the class will pay no attention if the topic is not to be tested.

Time

This dominance may appear in less spectacular forms, in the fact that the teacher or examiner will fix the timing, the duration, and the marking scheme of a test. Tests are carried out when teachers decide rather than when learners feel at their peak. Learners rarely have the chance to abort a test because they feel they have got off on the wrong foot and want to make a fresh start, though such fresh starts are perfectly normal when one is writing a letter or preparing a set of figures for one's work. As far as duration is concerned, writers on Transactional Analysis distinguish three kinds of time: **clock time** 'Work till nine o'clock and then stop'; **goal time** 'Finish this job and then stop'; and **hurry-up time** 'Finish the job by nine o'clock' (Berne 1974, p. 211). The first of these corresponds to what is known as a 'power test', one in which there are more items than any candidate could be expected to complete in the time limit, so that the rate of work is being measured as well as its accuracy. The second is hardly ever used in institutional testing. The third imposes the greatest stress, but it is overwhelmingly the most common.

The enjoyment of tests

And yet students love tests. You may find this hard to believe. The evidence that students hate tests is, of course, their groans when told that a test is due and their anxiety before a major examination. Clearly there is very little love on these occasions. But what the students dislike is the institutional consequences of a test, the need to revise, the tedious delay in getting results, and the risk of humiliation when results are given. Remove some or all of these factors and then the process of taking the test can turn into something stimulating and enjoyable. A course which contained no testing or feedback at all would quickly give rise to complaints.

The counter-evidence, that students love tests, is all around us; think of the sales of quiz books and games, the huge popularity of TV quiz shows, the enthusiasm with which people fill in quite complex questionnaires in magazines on such subjects as 'Do you take enough exercise?' or 'Assess your sex appeal', and the addictiveness of very ordinary tests and quizzes when they are provided on a microcomputer and the results not stored for use by outsiders.

Testing, therefore, is not inherently magisterial. One of the demands that the young master will often make of the pedagogue is 'Give me a test'. The motivation for this can be simply wanting success and approval; one is more likely to ask for a test when one is fairly confident of knowing most of the answers. But there is also a real curiosity to know one's standard, to have one's command externally assessed. Such assessments are all the more welcome if they are related to performance, if they tell you what types of activity you can now undertake with confidence.

Criterion and norm

In order to find out whether one has acquired enough skill to carry out a practical task, one must be able to relate the test result to some *criterion*, a score which is known to predict the real-life ability. Tests which have this characteristic are known as 'criterion-referenced'. They are not designed to rank people in ability order or relate them to some average, merely to provide evidence of a skill. They are often associated with *training* rather than with general education, for instance learning to drive or learning office skills rather than academic work. The pass mark in a criterion-referenced test is often very high, perhaps 90 per cent or 95 per cent, but the questions and tasks will be straightforward and 'easy' for anyone who has followed the training. This reflects the fact that the purpose of the test is to eliminate the lazy and the incompetent rather than to identify the elite. One normally expects the majority of people enrolled on a course of training to pass the final test; after all, each failure represents a wasted investment of time and effort.

In contrast to this, tests which belong in the realm of education rather than training serve a rather different purpose. General institutional education has a pyramid structure, with ever diminishing numbers passing from primary to secondary, from secondary to tertiary, and from undergraduate to graduate. However much politicians try to conceal it, public education is a rationed commodity which will be doled out to those selected. This leads to the use of 'norm-

referenced' tests which simply measure learners' performance in
relation to a given population. Their main purpose is to discriminate;
to make this easy, the pass mark is usually set at about the middle of
the range of marks, somewhere between 45 per cent and 60 per cent.
In terms of *training* this looks ludicrous: how can somebody 'pass' a
course if they have failed in half of the tasks which they are supposed
to be able to do? The answer is that norm-referenced tests usually
contain tasks and questions which go beyond what has been explicitly
taught. High scores show greater diligence or deeper perceptions
than the average; low scores may show laziness and incompetence,
but they may also show that a learner has been 'trapped' into studying
the wrong selection of facts or making wrong deductions. It is the
results of norm-referenced tests which are most open to charges of
'unfairness' or to complaints of 'bad luck'.

Fuzziness

And yet it is norm-referenced tests which give the strongest appearance of accuracy. Given a carefully constructed test and a large population on which to try it out, there are statistical techniques which
will produce detailed and stable measures of test performance (stable
for the whole population rather than for any individual). The reliability of the test can be calculated, raw scores converted to percentile
scores, and results displayed to several places of decimals. Computers
are nowadays being used more and more often to carry out the rather
tedious calculations involved, and unhappily the use of computers
tends to encourage belief in the 'rightness' of the calculations.
However, the accuracy of the machine conceals the fact that the
kinds of numbers thrown up by tests are 'fuzzy'.

Any test has an inevitable degree of unreliability: the student might
have got a different mark if he or she had had a different breakfast
or if the paper had been set or corrected by a different examiner.
From the reliability index (which could better be called the unreliability index) one can calculate the *standard error of measurement*, a
figure which gives a guide to the confidence one can place in an
individual's score. A test may have a standard error of, say, three
percentage points (by no means untypical even for well-validated
tests). What this means is that a student's 'true' score almost certainly
lies within three standard errors of the actual score: a student with
60 per cent almost certainly should have scored no worse than 51
per cent and no better than 69 per cent. There are nine chances out
of ten that the student's true score lies within two standard errors,

namely between 54 per cent and 66 per cent. There are only two chances in three (slightly better than the toss of a coin) that the true score is within one standard error, i.e. between 57 per cent and 63 per cent. Diagrammatically it looks like this:

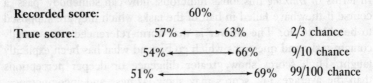

Recorded score: 60%

True score: 57% ⟷ 63%   2/3 chance

54% ⟷ 66%   9/10 chance

51% ⟷ 69%   99/100 chance

The trouble comes when you consider this in relation to the overlap with other students. Suppose the pass mark on a certain exam is 59 per cent with a standard error of three per cent, and we are comparing a group of students, all of whom have scored 50 per cent and have 'failed', with another group who have scored 60 per cent and who have 'passed'. Their scores differ by roughly three standard errors. The actual spread of their abilities as shown on a frequency chart would look something like this:

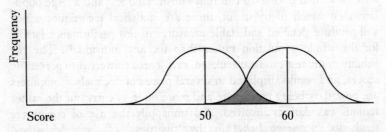

The shaded area represents the cases where there is at least an even chance that our pass/fail decision is wrong. In this case it is small compared with the whole distribution; probably only one in forty of these students have been misranked. But the picture looks rather different if we compare a failing group who have scored 57 per cent with the passing group with 60 per cent. This time the difference is only one standard error:

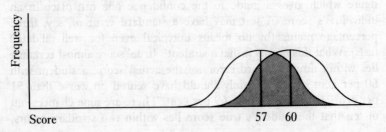

The shaded area now accounts for over half the total area under the curve, which can be taken to mean that more than one quarter of these students have been misranked. Considering how many important decisions, such as admission to university, may be made on the strength of small differences in exam scores, we need to remember that these decisions are gambles rather than certainties. The recorded score may be the only evidence we have, but it is flimsy evidence.

Parameters

Most of what has been said so far applies to the testing of any subject, but language testing adds a further level of difficulty. The problem is that we are trying to measure *command*, a set of subconscious abilities which we do not fully understand and which may well be subject to great fluctuation, and we can only measure it with indirect observations of behaviour. It is as if we were trying to judge a person's skill at walking, using only a small number of still photographs taken at widely separated times, and without a clear notion of how a 'good walker' is to be judged.

The difficulty lies in finding actual parameters to measure in the learner's *performance* which will tell us something useful about the underlying *competence*. The term 'parameter', by the way, is one which is often misused and misunderstood. It means 'numerical characteristic of a population', and has nothing to do with limits or boundaries. Three parameters are generally measured by language tests:

> *Quantity*, e.g. of words recognized, of grammatical structures manipulated, of phonological contrasts made, all these quantities being assessed by a sampling process.
>
> *Rates*, e.g. of words read per minute.
>
> *Density of error*, e.g. per page of writing or per minute of interview.

It is extremely difficult to find any parameter which is proportional to the central language skill of wanting to express a meaning and successfully encoding it. This is because you cannot inject a measured number of 'wants' into a student and then examine the success rate of encoding. Therefore there can be no true sampling. This is why it is far easier to measure comprehension than production, and why most measures of production are subjective impressions rather than objective counts.

Indirect measures

There is nothing wrong with using an indirect measure if one can be sure that it correlates well with the characteristic we are investigating. One can, for example, make a very good estimate of the weather in a seaside resort by using the figures for sales of ice cream. However, we know we can do this only because we have access for some resorts to both sets of data, and can therefore judge how close a fit there is between temperature fluctuations and the popularity of ice cream. In language testing we cannot make precise comparisons, since we lack hard data for the learners' competence, so that we cannot trust the indirect measures so well.

A great drawback of indirect measures is their lack of credibility. Somebody studying a holiday brochure would not trust the graph of ice-cream sales in the same way they would trust a table of readings from an actual thermometer. The technical term for this distrust is lack of *face validity*. Tests may be resented if the candidates cannot see how the tester is going to derive information from the test results. This was revealed very clearly in the case of a type of listening test which I call the 'hidden-word test', which was used in the sixties in at least one public examination but which now seems to have been dropped. In a hidden-word test the candidate hears a series of sentences. In my own versions of the test these sentences build up into a coherent story, but it is commoner to find isolated sentences being used. For each sentence the candidate sees four words and must choose the one which actually occurred in the sentence. For instance:

The candidate hears
  MR BROWN IS A TEACHER.

The candidate sees
  A: BROWNIE   B: ISN'T   C: A   D: TEA

The candidate hears
  HE LIVES IN A SMALL FLAT.

The candidate sees
  A: EEL   B: LIVES   C: SINNER   D: ALL

The candidate should choose answer C in the first item and B in the second, since only these words were used meaningfully in the sentences. The point of the test is that the distractors (the wrong answers) are all similar to sound sequences which occurred in the spoken sentences, though not as meaningful units. If the sentences are just a blur of sound, then any of the four words could have been 'heard'. It is only when students have successfully decoded the sentence, in a sense written it out in their minds, that the correct answer can be picked out reliably.

I used this form of test as one component of a college entry test used on large numbers of candidates in Turkey and later in Eygpt. Statistically it performed magnificently, with high reliability and a strong correlation with the total scores of each candidate. It predicted the candidate's result on the whole test much better than any of the other sub-tests. So why not use it more often? The answer was that there were too many complaints from students (and some from colleagues) who could not see what was being tested and who feared some subtle trap. I imagine it was dropped from the public examination on similar grounds.

Testing by task setting

Perhaps the best way of finding out if somebody commands a skill is simply to set a task in which the skill must be used and then see how well the task is carried out. Various attempts have been made to do this for language, most notably in recent years by the Royal Society of Arts team led by Keith Morrow which produced the *Examinations in the communicative use of English as a foreign language*, first administered in 1979. All these examinations are based on authentic material. Simulating tasks which involve listening, reading, and even writing, has posed no great problem. However, the RSA admit themselves that the oral interaction tasks pose formidable administrative problems (Royal Society of Arts 1981, p. 15).

In 1975 I experimented with a form of test which was based on counting items of information conveyed during an oral interaction. It involved two examiners, each in a separate room. The first had a sheet of paper in front of him which contained information in note form – either a house agent's description of a house for sale, or the application form of a candidate for a job. The candidate had five minutes in which to elicit through questions as much of this information as possible, and could take notes. He or she then proceeded to the second room where the second examiner was waiting with a sheet of thirty questions of detail. The scoring was based simply on the number of items of information successfully conveyed. This kind of test has a very high face validity; it appears to correspond to relevant real-life skills. However, the results were subject to distortion from practice effects. Students who had had a chance to work out a strategy for the questioning had an enormous advantage over those who took the test 'cold'. If the test had won wide acceptance, there would, therefore, have been a noticeable 'washback' effect on classroom preparation. The sheer cost and complexity of the format, however, ruled out its use on a large scale, and I had to abandon my experiment after one set of trials.

The ARELS test

Among the best tests of oral English ever devised have been those of the ARELS (Association of Recognized English Language Schools) organization. A good washback effect has always been an important part of the design of these tests; the examiners have tried to include only the kinds of questions which will encourage good teaching and relevant selection of topics. The tests are given in the form of a one-hour tape which has to be played in a language laboratory booth so that candidates can record their answers. The tapes are then sent in to the central office, cleverly copied so that the questions and instructions are stripped out leaving just the answers, and these short tapes, now about fifteen minutes long, are passed to assessors. There are comprehension questions, questions which require reading aloud in a realistic setting (e.g. passing on a message over the telephone, or reading a letter to somebody who has lost his glasses), and questions of the form 'What do you say when . . .?' The closest the examination comes to testing full oral interaction is in a type of question in which the candidate listens to a conversation, the conversation is interrupted from time to time, and the candidate is prompted to speak with a line such as 'What do you think, Pat? Is Pete's father being unreasonable or not?' Even this ingenious device is not realistic enough. It has not injected a real wish to communicate, and my impression as an assessor was always that the students' answers were calculated rather than spontaneous.

Profiles

Since it is so difficult to get direct measures of *command*, the best we can do is to call up all the indirect measures available to us, using the common-sense assumption that large samples provide a better basis for prediction than small ones. We get better information if we examine a variety of measures, subjective and objective, rather than trying to derive a single number to measure global ability. After all, we know more about a person's physique if we know their height *and* weight *and* waist measurement rather than just one of these numbers or a single figure derived from all three. There is nowadays a great interest in 'profile testing', which combines information from different tests into a profile of different skills and applications. We could, for instance, separate Listening, Speaking, Reading and Writing, and produce a profile of a student which looks like this:

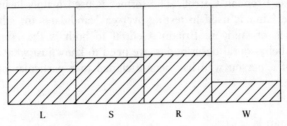

We could also produce a profile of a job specification, say that of waiter in a tourist hotel:

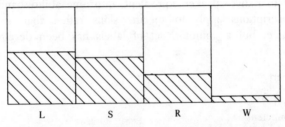

If we superimpose the job profile on the student profile, we get an approximate measure of what skills the student needs to acquire if he or she is to perform the duties of the job, and we may then try to turn this into a syllabus specification or an estimate of the amount of tuition needed.

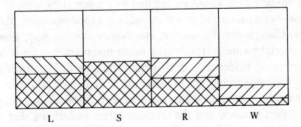

Bands

So far the profiles have not carried any scales. To make them useful we have to quantify the distance between perfection at the top and total incompetence at the bottom, and then describe what we mean by all the intermediate points. There have been two important attempts to do this. The first was ELTDU's Scale of Attainment

Battery developed under the guidance of John Webb. The second was the British Council's Banding Scheme, the principal architect of which was Brendan Carroll. The former is used mainly in industry, while the latter is used in testing overseas candidates for admission to courses of study in Britain. Central to both is the concept of detailed behavioural descriptions: we need to know just what we can expect of a person who has been assigned to a particular point on the scale.

Ability bands

The British Council scheme divides the whole ability range, from total beginner to native-speaker equivalent, into nine ability bands. The band descriptions apply to specific skills rather than to global competence, but a common set of labels has been developed as follows:

9 Expert
8 High level
7 Good
6 Competent
5 Modest
4 Marginal
3 Limited
2 Intermittent
1 Non-

Each of these labels would be applied to a noun suggesting the skill which has been measured or estimated, e.g. Good Speaker, Marginal Listener, Competent Translator, etc. Notice, by the way, that level 0 has a special meaning. It does not mean that no skill is present, only that there is no evidence, e.g. that the candidate did not turn up for the test. We need to beware of using the scale naively. For one thing, it is not an even-interval scale: the difference between a band 8 and a band 7 performance and the learning effort underlying that difference is greater than that between bands 3 and 2, for instance. This simply reflects the fact that progress is more easily perceived at elementary levels. There is also a danger in using a numbered scale in that it suggests that learning is a smooth linear process rather than the lurchingly complex one it really is, and this danger is greatest if we try to apply band numbers to global ability rather than to performance at specific skills. Each of the nine bands is associated with a set of behavioural descriptions. (For samples, see Carroll 1980, pp. 134–9.) The descriptions may be highly detailed, occupying a page or more for each band level at each skill, or they may consist of one or two lines to summarize each band. They may include technical specifications or be written entirely in layman's language. The purpose is to give the reader a mental picture of what a typical student at each band level will be like. It is, of course, important to spread these descriptions as widely as possible; they need to be developed into a common reference standard between students, teachers, testers and employers, so that each of them, hearing the words 'Band Five' can immediately form a mental picture of the kind of ability associated with that level. The nine bands can be very roughly approximated to existing labels, as follows:

9

Advanced ◄──── { 8   Overseas degree
                   7   CPE, Overseas teacher-training certificate

Intermediate ◄──── { 6   Cambridge FCE
                      5   Council of Europe Threshhold

Elementary ◄──── { 4   Council of Europe Waystage
                    3   Council of Europe Survival

Beginner ◄──── { 2   Council of Europe Basic Survival
                  1

It must be emphasized that these equivalences are only very approximate.

It is well worth any teacher's while to try to develop a feel for bands. Study some published band descriptions, and try them out in discussions with colleagues, by making assessments of yourself in different skill areas, your students, and public figures who perform in foreign languages in the media. Start throwing around terms like 'Band Four' in order to stimulate discussion and exemplification, so that the common reference standard develops. There is also no reason why your students should not be brought in on the act. Give them band descriptions to look at, and encourage them to estimate their own band levels. Where their own estimates differ from yours, there should be fruitful grounds for discussion.

Discriminatory power

Band descriptions can be used directly as aids in making subjective evaluations, e.g. in interviews or essay marking, and experienced testers can usually be relied on to make judgements which are *reliable* within one band. However, the result is relatively coarse, with many students sharing the same score. This approach is most appropriate in a wide-ranging form of evaluation, such as placement testing for an institute, or screening of applicants for study places, in which hopeful near beginners may present themselves alongside well-qualified advanced students. In most kinds of test, however, the task is to discriminate among a narrower ability range. If a class contains both a band 8 and a band 2 student, whatever the skill, something must have gone wrong with the selection process. For this reason, it is usually best to make a realistic assessment of the probable extremes before evaluating performances of the members of one class. In an elementary class, for instance, one is unlikely to meet performances outside the range of band 2 to band 5. Having set such limits, one can adopt scales which allow one to use whatever discriminatory power one has efficiently.

The staggered scale

There is psychological evidence that the most efficient way to record impressions or to make holistic judgements is to use a five-point scale. If asked to use a wider scale, most of us operate within a limited portion of the scale. Asked to use a ten-point scale, for instance, most people will give no mark higher than eight or lower than two, thus turning the ten-point scale into a seven-point one. However, decisions about language performance are often disturbed by a feeling that performances are not comparable, i.e. that a linear scale is not the appropriate way to measure. I would suggest a modification of the five-point scale for most forms of subjective evaluation, as follows:

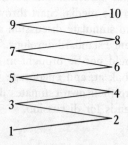

On this scale one is making two decisions: firstly, is the performance on the whole characterized by risk taking and fluency (symbolized by the use of odd numbers), or by caution and accuracy (symbolized by the use of even numbers); secondly, where does this performance lie on a five-point scale? Thus a performance judged as 5 can be regarded as an enterprising 4 or an inaccurate 6. A performance judged as 6 is either an accurate 5 or an over-cautious 7. This provides an answer to the perennial problem of looking at two essays of roughly the same standard, one of which is long and ambitious but full of errors, and the other short and limited but correct within its limits.

The student as evaluator

What I have written in the last paragraph may suggest that subjective or impression marking is entirely in the domain of the teacher or testing expert, but there is no compelling reason why this should be so. Students are not generally very good at judging their own work, but they get very little practice. Given the chance, they can become a great deal better at it. In the seventies, and particularly in Sweden and France, a good deal of work was done on self-assessment (see Oskarsson 1980). Much of this work was intended for students using self-access resources, but was no less relevant to students following taught courses. It deserves to be better known. Self-assessment, of course, sits very uneasily in a magisterial context, since one feels one could not rely on the students' judgement or honesty. 'What is to stop them cheating?' Nothing, of course, except the learners' gradual discovery that they do not wish to and get no advantage from it. The whole object of self-assessment, however, is not to supply data for external use, but to train students to become interested in, and ultimately good at, knowing themselves.

One interesting experiment, proposed by Frank Smith (1983), is to ask students to estimate their own passive vocabulary, the number of words which they would not need to look up if they encountered them in a passage which they were required to read or translate. Their first estimate is likely to be quite low. Now give them a dictionary and ask them to note a given word, say the headword at the top left of each page. Out of fifty such headwords, how many do they know? Then multiply this number as a proportion of fifty by the number of words listed in the dictionary. (You can usually find out how many words there are in a dictionary by looking at the preface to see the total number of entries and then reducing this number by about a third to take account of separate entries for verb and noun pairs like *walk* and other close synonyms or derived forms, such as *cream* the colour and *cream* the substance.) This will give them a reasonable estimate of the size of their passive vocabulary. This is usually a good deal higher than their first informal estimate, and it can give quite a boost to their confidence to find out that they know more than they thought they knew.

Discussing test results

Even with conventional classroom tests students can be invited to predict their test results. If their prediction fails to match the actual result, they will want to find out the reasons. Obviously, this depends on quick feedback; it will be no good giving them the result after an interval of days, or even hours, since they will have forgotten what made them answer as they did. If they discuss the results with the teacher, it becomes very important for the teacher to function as pedagogue. If advice and explanation are mixed up with magisterial exhortations to work harder, then the desire for enlightenment may be destroyed.

One very practical way of combining a pedagogue's instant feedback with a magister's record-keeping function was suggested to me by the distinguished Yugoslav methodologist, Eva Kraus-Srebić. When she gives a class test, she hands out to each student two sheets of paper and a sheet of carbon paper. At the end of the test the top copy is collected and marked at leisure. Students can now discuss the answers they gave and ask for explanations of any mistakes or difficulties.

Addictive tests

The popularity and addictiveness of simple quizzes and tests on computers is something which surprises and to some extent appals those who, like the present author, want to see computers used in a more imaginative way in education. I think we have to recognize the motivating power of scoring and the competitive instinct (not only competition with others but also with oneself). Perhaps, too, students know better than us what is good for them. Computer tests are, after all, a form of exposure to language, and what is encountered in them may as readily be retained as what is encountered in teachers' presentations (as is well demonstrated in Jones 1983). The lesson for the classroom teacher would seem to be to give lots of informal tests, particularly those which can be marked rapidly, preferably by the students themselves. In the informal situation of the class, convey the idea that tests can be fun, and that the results are interesting. But one should also encourage a proper scepticism about the actual scores

and their interpretation. If we have learned to regard numbers as
'fuzzy', we should pass the lesson on to the learners.

Security

Institutional testing in general and norm-referenced testing in
particular have always been bedevilled by problems of security.
Students will try to cheat. The test, it seems, is regarded as a contest
and, as in other forms of contest such as love and war, all means are
regarded as 'fair'. Cheating means only that the learner perceives the
test as magisterial, i.e. administered at somebody else's behest and for
somebody else's benefit. The test setter may find this deplorable, but
no amount of exhortation is likely to lead to a change of heart.

The computer, with its ability to undertake tasks which are
drudgery to humans, can make quite a difference to security. Given
a bank of validated items, it can make up the test by random selection
of items, and, if there are enough items, it can produce several parallel
forms of the test so that candidates sitting together are not looking
at the same paper. With a multiple-choice test it can print right
answers and distractors in a random order, producing the answer key
only after the test is taken. This may produce distortions in the
reliability of particular items, but the effect should even itself out over
a long test. I also suspect that the use of special answer sheets
prepared for machine scanning may scare some students from cheating
in case the computer is able in some mysterious way to identify the
answers in which cheating occurred. It is significant that, in a 1983
survey of overseas teaching institutes conducted by the British
Council, a large number in the Third World put 'test security' as one
of their major reasons for wanting a computer.

Guessing

An interesting sidelight is cast on the magister/pedagogue distinction
by the topic of guessing. The traditional attitude of the magisterial
teacher was to deplore guessing, to say sternly to a student: 'You
didn't know that, you just guessed.' Guessing was virtually equated
with cheating. Most teachers now would agree that intelligent
guessing is a perfectly legitimate way of arriving at a correct answer
and a good score. Another lesson we can draw from quiz-addictive-
ness is the power and appeal of guessing. Guessing is very rarely
completely 'blind', and developing a readiness to guess may well be
a means of developing useful language skills.

Graded objectives

It would be a tragic missed opportunity if the availability of computers led to the perpetuation of mass testing at fixed times, using indirect norm-referenced measures yielding single figures to represent 'global' ability. A far better development would be in the direction of the 'graded objectives' movement, already endorsed by a number of education authorities in Britain. This is an attempt to make the examining of foreign languages into something resembling the examining of musical ability. Tests are as far as possible authentic and based on tasks or on simulations of tasks. The timing is flexible, so that candidates take the test when they are ready rather than at a fixed age or even a fixed time of year. Above all, the marking is criterion-referenced and is related to published behavioural descriptions, so that everybody can find out just what each grade promises in terms of skill. Although it has turned out in practice to be very difficult to cover the whole ability range in this way, it is worth continuing the attempt. The Graded Objectives movement is the closest approach to a pedagogue's role rather than a magister's in institutionalized testing.

Computers and testing

The computer in educational institutions serves the magister, not the pedagogue. It stores data and calculates scores, and may even be the direct medium for taking the test if the institution is rich enough to afford a bank of machines for the purpose. But such uses make only trivial demands on computer power. In order to exploit it more, we first have to educate the learners into calling on the pedagogue. Once they acquire the habit of asking questions about their own performance, we can begin to move computer testing out of the area of data processing and into that of expert systems.

Expert systems

An expert system is an attempt to simulate the decision-making processes of a human expert who collects data, some of which may be confused and contradictory, and then makes an informed judgement. Successful expert systems have been developed in such areas as medical diagnosis and oil prospecting. Human experts may be unable to describe the processes used to reach their decisions, ascribing them in part to 'feel'. This feel arises from a weight of experience which leads the expert to give different weightings to different kinds of data and to look for certain types of evidence to be associated. It may be too complex to be made explicit, just as the way we produce and understand language may be too complex to be made fully explicit. The computer's expert system replaces the unconscious 'feel' with a technique of assigning probabilities to data, but making sure that the probability values are changed whenever a prediction fails. Thus it learns from its own mistakes and acquires a body of 'experience'.

In language testing we can easily acquire and feed to the computer a body of norm-referenced data, expectations that certain kinds of performance show the learners' rank order position among a certain population. What we will need to do instead is to equip the machine to make criterion-referenced judgements, for example to say, after measuring the learners' recognition of a given vocabulary and their ability to infer meaning from a set of short texts, whether they are now capable of using untranslated workshop manuals in their technical field. In due course it may be possible for a computer to make more comprehensive judgements, such as whether a learner is ready to work as a clerk or to begin undergraduate study in a given subject. We need to be cautious about this, however. There are so few human experts who can do this reliably, that we may need to discover more about the nature of that particular expertise before we try to embody it in a computerized expert system.

The human window

Such gross judgements will only be possible after we have accumulated a mass of experience with smaller and less crucial judgements, predictions and associations. In the process we can expect to find out a great deal about the connections between certain features of performance and certain types of command. It will be important to maintain the 'human window': in other words it must always be possible to ask the machine to state the evidence and to explain the reasons for its judgements, and to get an answer in an intelligible form (see Michie and Johnston 1984, p. 71).

Adaptive testing

Meanwhile it may be possible to take some steps on the way towards an expert system through the process known as adaptive testing. This is not a new idea. There are many institutions which have used a paper-and-pencil form of adaptive testing for placement, and the Nelson Quicktest is a published example of the technique. That test comes as a four-page folder. All candidates answer the questions on page one, and this is scored immediately by the supervisor using an overlay. According to the score, each candidate is directed to tackle page two, three or four. Their score on that page becomes their final score, unless it is very high, in which case they get the chance to do the next page (assuming they have not already reached page four). This means that candidates only answer those sections of the test which will yield the largest amount of information about their standard.

The responsiveness and elaborate data-handling capacities of computers can enrich this process, allowing the tester to probe certain areas of the candidate's performance in depth while disregarding those in which the candidate is clearly competent or incompetent. But there is a danger that the machine will be credited with more power than it has. The machine can process the information but cannot 'understand' the questions it is asking or know the reasons for the student's right or wrong answers. Adaptive testing, like any other form of testing, depends on well-thought-out objectives, well-written items and tasks, proper validation, and sensitive interpretation.

Conclusion

It has been said that the computer is fast, accurate, and stupid. Humans are slow, inaccurate, and brilliant. When they are able to combine effectively, the results will be unimaginable. Nowhere will this apply more strongly than in the area of our awareness of ourselves. A language-testing expert system may in the end reveal to us a great deal that we do not yet understand about language and how it is learned, but we still have a long time to wait before we are ready to create one.

7 The machine

You know, in ten years' time we're going to look back at this conference [The Use of Computers in the Teaching of Chemistry] and think 'What a silly title!' It's as if we were to have a conference on the use of paper in the teaching of chemistry.

John Crookes (Lancaster University), Ljubljana, 1985

A very common question raised at conferences and courses is this: 'How do we know that the computer is not going to be as disappointing as the language laboratory?' The questioners usually follow this up with a paraphrase of advertisers' claims for the language laboratory and accounts of misused and abandoned laboratories in schools they know.

One reason this question is wide of the mark is that it is not comparing like with like. A computer nowadays is a small, portable, flexible device which does not cost a great deal of money. A better comparison would be with the tape-recorder. Suppose we rephrase the question: 'How do we know that the computer is not going to be as disappointing as the tape-recorder?' Now surely there will be somebody who will jump up to say that the tape-recorder has not been a disappointment, that it has enabled fragments of authentic and exciting spoken discourse to be brought into the classroom, that it has provided models of native speech, using a variety of speakers, that it has given opportunities for spoken homework and project work, or that it has given learners a chance to hear themselves as they really sound when talking the foreign language.

In defence of the laboratory

Then we might find people to tell us that all of these things could be done with the language laboratory as well as with single tape-recorders. From quite early there were teachers who were ready to use their laboratories mainly as listening stations, with commercial or off-air recordings of drama or news bulletins. There were teachers who provided open-ended activities in which students gave their own responses and had the satisfaction of listening to themselves apparently taking part in a foreign-language conversation. There were teachers who used the jigsaw-listening principle, asking students to listen to different and incomplete accounts of the same event, so that they had to fill in the gaps afterwards by asking other members of the class what they had heard. There were even some teachers who made their students move from booth to booth, picking up information left by the last occupant and contributing more of their own.

The investment burden

So what went wrong? Why has the language laboratory, which is nothing more than a battery of tape-recorders linked to a control console, not come to be regarded as a way to make language learning more interesting, more realistic and more successful? Why instead is it so often associated with boredom and failure? There are a number of reasons, one of which is the burden of guilt associated with any very large cash investment, the thought of that machine, which has cost thousands of pounds, being used frivolously or sporadically rather than regularly and coherently. This led to the development and distribution of courseware packages, material designed so that each class hour could be supported by half an hour of drill, whether or not half an hour was what the learners wanted or needed at that moment. It is when these failed to work well, or led to complaints from the students, or even vandalizing of the equipment, that laboratory work was sometimes abandoned and the machine left to gather dust. The commonest excuse was that the machine had gone wrong or spare parts could not be supplied. Such excuses are nonsense, of course. If a machine is known to be performing a valuable function, one can always find somebody who can maintain and repair it, or at worst replace it with another machine which works properly.

The Sorcerer's Apprentice

Another reason for the abandonment of laboratories is the distrust and fear of machinery which affects all of us. Machines which we do not fully understand and think we cannot control will arouse in us the kind of fear described in the fairy tale 'The Sorcerer's Apprentice'. The apprentice wanted to use his master's magic broom to do the household chores, but he discovered that, although he could command it to start, he could not remember the magic words to stop it, and the broom gradually swept everything out of the house.

We are now familiar enough with the keys of a portable tape-recorder, but the console of a language laboratory or the keyboard of a computer are things we may shy away from precisely because we are afraid of losing control, perhaps damaging an expensive device or, at best, being made to look foolish when the technician has to be called. The laboratory, therefore, tended to become the province of a specialist, somebody who had tamed the beast, or else something to be used in a completely regular way with the teacher in charge following a well-rehearsed routine to copy out the week's drills to the student positions. In place of individualization, one of the laboratory's greatest advantages, there was the lockstep approach, everybody in the class carrying out the same assignment because it was too difficult to provide different tapes for each learner. The majority of English teachers were not encouraged or trained to use the laboratory experimentally. It was no wonder, then, that they did not agitate for replacement of unserviceable equipment; on the contrary, they were generally delighted to be relieved of the need to use it.

Fear of authenticity

There is, perhaps, a third reason, one which is not aired so often. During the sixties and seventies laboratories were presented in numbers to institutions in developing countries. Although they were usually free gifts, they were often given as much to provide outlets for the over-stocked electronics industry of the donor country as to meet any real need. Local teachers were rarely consulted, but generally welcomed the machines on their first arrival because of the aura of modernity and the resulting enhanced prestige of the subject. Once the machines were in place, however, they discovered that authenticity, even the watered-down authenticity of actors reading drills and dialogues, can threaten the *status quo* of the classroom.

Of all the people who teach English worldwide, probably no more than a fifth are native speakers. Another fifth, perhaps, are confident and accomplished users of the language, able to speak and write fluently with very few errors and able to diagnose any errors their students make in free conversation. The remainder cover a wide range of performance but share a common anxiety, uncertainty about whether usages which they have not heard before are or are not correct. One way of avoiding this uncertainty is to stay rigidly within the syllabus. I have come across one teacher who took this to the point of banning dictionaries of any kind, and confiscating them if they were brought into the classroom: her students would only be allowed to learn what she taught them. What the language laboratory did was to face such teachers and their students with evidence of a difference between what the teacher sounded like and what the native speaker sounded like. At the level of pronunciation this did not matter too much; one could reasonably claim that the target level for pronunciation was intelligibility rather than mimicry. At the level of grammar it was potentially devastating.

It therefore became important to remove this dangerous element of authenticity, and that may account for the many recording projects that took place in the seventies, producing quite unnecessary drill packages. The recordings were often made with a mixture of native speakers and local teachers (I have taken part in many such recording sessions myself), but the words they had to say were taken exclusively from the local syllabus or a locally written textbook. The laboratory was being turned into a device to stop learners learning what they were not supposed to learn, rather than a learning aid.

Separation

Another response to the threat was to separate the laboratory work from classwork, and this was aided by the design of the laboratory itself. The locked room was often remote from the regular classroom and could only be visited at fixed times. The booths isolated each learner from other human contacts. The work itself was often different, and used a different set of books which were stored in the laboratory and never removed. Although trainers gave lectures and experts wrote articles about integrating language laboratory work with classwork, it turned out that integration was not what many teachers wanted. On the contrary, they were quite content to maintain a physical and philosophical separation between what happened in the classroom and the closed world of the laboratory, since that made the linguistic differences less glaring.

The computer as language laboratory

These three factors, then, led to the decline and widespread rejection of the language laboratory: the burden of a large cash investment, the fear of a complex machine, and the clash between the comfortable limitations of a syllabus and the disturbing uncertainty of real discourse. How many of these are likely to affect the computer? The first may have an effect if education systems invest in computer configurations resembling the laboratory, in other words special locked rooms containing multiple machines with central control. But, since the computer is a general purpose machine, these investments are not going to be made by language departments. The computer laboratories will be there, but they will belong to the school as a whole, or else to the physics and maths departments; language teachers will use them only when they want to and when they can be allocated time. The guilt burden of having to fill the timetable with systematic computer work should not affect them.

The second factor, fear of complex machinery, will be strong for a while but is bound to diminish with time. Computers acquired specifically for language learners are more likely to be stand-alone micros or stations on a network system, i.e. connected to a central facility but not in the same room as all the others. Such equipment may still be daunting to many teachers; the parable of the Sorcerer's Apprentice remains powerful. But, as the machines become more and more commonplace (and they will spread as rapidly in the Third World as they have in Europe) they are bound to lose their mystique. Meanwhile software writers and system designers are showing ever greater ingenuity in making programs easy to use without diminishing the variety of material and tasks. Computers, having far fewer moving parts than language laboratories, are already proving much more reliable and durable, so the excuse that the machines are out of order and cannot be repaired will be harder to sustain.

Authentic discourse

That leaves the third factor, the way in which the machine exposes the anxious teacher to damaging comparisons with authentic discourse. This is not going to diminish; on the contrary, it is likely to have a far greater effect than it did in the case of the language laboratory. Since the laboratory was a speech medium, both learners and teachers were able to ignore to some extent those parts of the discourse which did not fit in with their grammatical expectations; some research I carried out in 1975 demonstrated how often students in language laboratories 'heard' what they expected to hear rather than the actual words recorded on the tape in the correction phase of a drill (Higgins 1975). Computers, however, display written forms and often demand accurate entry of language before you can proceed with an activity. The trial-and-error processes involved in, for instance, text reconstruction or exploratory programs may force both teachers and learners to 'debug' some of their grammatical rules and ideas about collocations and idioms. For some teachers this will be an upsetting experience.

The hermetic machine

Some teachers and school systems will respond as they did in the language laboratory era; they will create materials which stay within the syllabus and which do not allow much experiment. They may, too, separate periods of computer work from normal work so that it is perceived as something external to the normal processes of learning. This will entail using the computer in a magisterial way, carrying out drills and issuing corrections, since letting the machine be a pedagogue might encourage learners to experiment and, thus, to discover things they are not supposed to know. The old excuse will be trotted out, namely that pupils have to pass examinations and there is no time for work which is unrelated to the exam syllabus. The end result will be pupils who, whether they pass or not, have learned a great deal less than they were capable of learning, and teachers whose function and self-esteem is unthreatened.

The fallible teacher

Most teachers are seen by their classes as more or less infallible on points of fact relating to the subject matter they teach. If not infallible, then they are expected to be right most of the time. What is more, they are expected to sound right, to speak with certainty. This is not the result of any deliberate claims that individual teachers make, rather of the expectations set up in the whole education system. However, if one is going to use computers as tools rather than as delivery systems for software written to practise specific points of language, then surprises, uncertainties and problems are unavoidable. Perhaps the only kind of teacher who can cope with them is the one who is prepared not to be thought of as infallible. In an influential article published in 1983, Peter Medgyes suggested that teachers should not present themselves as people who have 'finished' learning but rather as advanced learners who can guide their pupils but can also share with them in the exploration and discovery of new language facts. He was not talking about computers at all, but what he says has even greater relevance for the teacher planning to introduce any form of machinery into the classroom (Medgyes 1983).

The fallible machine

One of the consequences of using the computer magisterially is that the machine, like the magisterial teacher, takes on an aura of infallibility. The right answers are stored and there is no appealing against a right/wrong decision. When computers are tools, however, one ceases to respect them in this way, and one can even find educational value in criticizing them. Learners may need a little nudging before they start criticizing, but can do it with zest once they see how few clothes the Emperor is wearing. Two examples will illustrate how a machine can sometimes be of more service if it does something badly rather than well.

Pocket translators

If you have a hundred pounds or so to spend, you can buy a gadget, the size of a pocket calculator, which claims to translate between languages. In fact it probably claims to be an accomplished polyglot, offering you a choice of a dozen different language chips to plug in at an extra thirty pounds a time. It has a forty-character keypad and a sixteen-character display. You can enter a word or phrase and the machine will search its memory for a translation, or you can browse through its repertoire, calling up the foreign-language equivalents of any words you are interested in. The size of the vocabulary may be up to two thousand words, and some of the machines also have a store of twenty or more useful sentence patterns into which the words can be inserted.

Is such a device an educational aid? When these machines are reviewed in the press, the reviewer usually delights in the howlers the machine makes and advises teachers to have nothing to do with them. Yet I know of several teachers who have used them in class precisely because they are imperfect. When the students have tried them out, the teacher asks them to predict the way the machine will translate a phrase, and to try to find common sentences which the machine is likely to get wrong. I know of one teacher, Joseph Rézeau, who uses the translation service offered by the French public database service MINITEL in precisely this way.

Speech chips

Many small computers can now be equipped with speech chips which make sounds approximating roughly to English vowels and consonants. The consonants are usually much less realistic than the vowels, but neither sound very natural. One can put these together to make words and phrases, and there may be a way to vary the pitch so that one can make an attempt to add intonation. One gets the machine to speak by entering certain letters and letter combinations, but one will have to learn the special conventions used by the programmer. Each sound corresponds to a phoneme or major allophone of English, and there will probably be at least sixty of them to choose from. Simply entering words in normal spelling will not be good enough; type in 'pike', for instance, and the machine will say something like 'pickay'.

Teachers often laugh at these gadgets, since they cannot provide a model of spoken English which students should copy. They may lose sight of another way of using them, namely as the raw material for simple experiments in phonetics. Intermediate students actually know reasonably well what English should sound like; they may not be able to produce a good accent themselves or to describe one, but they are often better than we imagine at recognizing one. What I have sometimes done is set a group of learners the task of teaching the machine to utter a sentence in as English a way as possible. The group usually begins by typing in ordinary spellings, and this alerts them at once to the difference between phonetics and orthography. With the aid of the machine's handbook and its look-up table of sound/spelling correspondences, they usually take five or ten minutes to come up with a version which is just intelligible. Now I suggest some possible modifications, doubling a letter to lengthen a sound, or using a different allophone, or inserting or deleting short stretches of silence, or varying the pitch. They continue to play around with the sentence for a few more minutes. Then I might play them the final version arrived at by another group, and they discuss whose version is more realistic. They may use me as a model, but all the time they are comparing the mechanical sound with a mental model of the English sentence. There is no danger that they will 'learn' the Dalek-like speech of the machine.

Artificial unintelligence

Anyone who works in the field of artificial intelligence quickly loses any awe they may feel towards the machinery, but they tend to gain in respect for the miracles of human mental powers. In fields such as vision and pattern recognition humans perform effortlessly tasks which machines perform laboriously and inaccurately. The power and flexibility with which humans handle language is still only feebly imitated by computer systems. The value to us of the unintelligent machine is that it applies rules rigorously, something that humans are not good at. It can show us in detail what language would be like if some of the simple rules we believe in were true. In both the applications I have just described, the translating machine and the speaking machine, the computer's failure was used to arouse interest in language itself. Used this way computers do not 'teach' language any more than the retorts and Bunsen burners of the school science laboratory can be said to 'teach' chemistry, but they can still play a part in helping people to learn language.

A laboratory is a place in which we can conduct experiments. The computer could well be called the new language laboratory. Interpreted pessimistically, this means it is the new means of delivering decontextualized practice activities in vast quantities and in a pseudo-individualized form (but now in writing rather than in speech). Interpreted optimistically it means that the computer turns the language classroom into an experimental environment, a place to try out ways of communicating or ways of manipulating grammar, and to study the effects, a place to collect samples of authentic usage (e.g. through a concordance), and derive principles and rules from the data.

To return to the question at the beginning of this chapter, will the computer as a language-learning aid be as great a disappointment as the language laboratory was? The answer depends not on the nature of the machine but on how people decide to use it. We can swamp computers with exposition and exercises, using them to carry an outdated and discredited form of teaching, or we can use their power to extend and satisfy our own natural inquisitiveness and desire to communicate. My own prediction is that computers will gradually enter language classrooms in their most menial roles, as word-processor, as database, as concordance, and will soon get taken for granted. In ten years' time we will look back on this debate and wonder what the fuss was about.

Bibliography

Berne, E 1974 *What do you say after you say Hello?* Corgi Books

Bright, J and McGregor, G 1970 *Teaching English as a second language.* Longman

Brumfit, C J 1983 Classrooms as language communities. In Holden, S (ed.) *Focus on the learner.* Modern English Publications

Carroll, B 1980 *Testing communicative performance.* Pergamon Press, Oxford

Cousin, W D 1983 *Computer Clozentropy: phase one report.* Scottish Centre for Education Overseas, Moray House, Edinburgh

Darnell, D K 1968 *The development of an English language proficiency test using clozentropy procedure.* Final report, US Dept of Health Education and Welfare, Project No BR 7-H-010. Colorado University, Boulder

Ellis, R 1985 *Understanding second language acquisition.* Oxford University Press

Farrington, B 1986 Computer assisted learning or computer inhibited acquisition? In Cameron, Dodd and Rahtz (eds.) *Computers and modern language studies*: 85–92. Ellis Horwood, Chichester

Higgins, J J 1981 CALL: the nature of the interaction. The British Council, unpublished mimeo

Higgins, J J 1975 Problems of self-correction in the language laboratory. *System* 3(3): 145–56

Higgins, J J 1983a Computer assisted language learning. *Language Learning* 16(2): 102–14

Higgins, J J 1983b Can computers teach? *Calico Journal* (Utah) 1(2): 4–6

Higgins, J J 1984 Learning with computers. In *Teaching and the teacher: proceedings of the Bologna Conference, April 1984*: 83–6. Modern English Publications

Higgins, J J 1986a Artificial unintelligence. In Pedersen and Spaeth (eds.) *EDB i fremmedsprak*: 32–40. Systime, Herning, Denmark

Higgins, M F 1981 Student power and the BOOH factor. Entry in the 1981 ESU competition, unpublished

Howatt, A P R 1969 *Programmed learning and the language teacher.* Longman

Johns, T F 1982 Exploratory CAL: an alternative use of the computer in teaching foreign languages. In Higgins J J (ed.) *CALL: British Council inputs*: 49–56

Johns, T F 1986 Micro-concord: a language learners' research tool. *System* **14**(2): 151–62

Jones, C 1983 Computer assisted language learning: testing or teaching? *English Language Teaching Journal* **37**(4): 247–50

Jones, C 1982 *Clozemaster.* Wida Software

Kelly, L G 1969 *25 centuries of language teaching.* Newbury House, Rowley, Massachusetts

Kemmis, S, Atkin, R and Wright, E 1977 How do students learn? *Working papers on computer-assisted learning: UNCAL Evaluation Studies.* Centre for Applied Research in Education, Occasional Publications No 5. Norwich

Krashen, S D 1982 *Principles and practice in second language acquisition.* Pergamon Press, Oxford

Medgyes, P 1983 The schizophrenic teacher. *English Language Teaching Journal* **37**(1): 2–6

Michie, D and Johnston, R 1984 *The creative computer.* Pelican Books

Moore, P 1986 *Using computers in English: a practical guide.* Methuen

O'Shea, T and Self, J 1983 *Learning and teaching with computers: artificial intelligence in education.* Harvester Press, Brighton

Oskarsson, M 1980 *Approaches to self-assessment in foreign language learning.* Pergamon Press, Oxford

Papert, S 1980 *Mindstorms: children, computers, and powerful ideas.* Harvester Press, Brighton

Rinvolucri, M 1985 Computer ideas for the chalkboard classroom. *Practical English Teaching* **5**(8)

Royal Society of Arts 1981 *Examinations in the communicative use of English as a foreign language: syllabus and specimen papers.*

Smith, F 1983 The promise and threat of microcomputers. *On TESOL 1984*

Weizenbaum, J 1976 *Computer power and human reason.* W H Freeman, San Francisco

Index